"Perfect for any film enthusiast looking for the secrets behind creating film… it is a great addition to the collection of students and film pros alike."
Ross Otterman
Directed By magazine

*"*Setting Up Your Shots *is a great book for defining the shots of today. The storyboard examples on every page make it a valuable reference book for directors and DP's alike! Great learning tool. Should be a boon for writers who want to choose the most effective shot and clearly show it in their boards for the maximum impact."*
Paul Clatworthy
Creator of Storyboard Artist and Storyboard Quick software

"This book is for both beginning and experienced filmmakers. It's a great reference tool, a quick reminder of the most commonly used shots by the greatest filmmakers of all time."
Cory Williams
President, Alternative Productions

Setting Up Your Shots

Great Camera Moves Every Filmmaker Should Know

Published by Michael Wiese Productions, 11288 Ventura Blvd., Suite 821,
Studio City, CA 91604, (818) 379-8799 Fax (818) 986-3408.
E-mail: wiese@earthlink.net
http://www.mwp.com

Cover design by The Art Hotel

Printed and Manufactured in the United States of America

ISBN 0-941188-73-6

Library of Congress Cataloging-in-Publication Data

Vineyard, Jeremy, 1977-
          Setting up your shots: great camera moves every filmmaker should know / by
Jeremy Vineyard.
                    p.   cm.
          Includes index.
          ISBN 0-941188-73-6
          1. Cinematography.   I. Title.
          TR850. V56   1999   99-38020
          778.5'3--dc21   CIP

ACKNOWLEDGMENTS

I would like to thank those who contributed to the content of this book with their ideas, comments, and suggestions: Jose Cruz, Stephen Greenfield, Alon Hartuv, JD Cochran, and Chris Huntley. I would especially like to thank Jose Cruz for donating so much of his time over the last year to create his excellent illustrations.

I found the Internet Movie Database to be invaluable when researching this book. The IMDB is an on-line database with information about thousands of films, television shows, actors, directors, writers, and more. The Internet address for their Web site is: www.imdb.com.

Also, thanks to the video rental chains out there that carry foreign films and alternative fare. Watching movies is kept interesting by their selections.

HOW TO USE THIS BOOK

If you are a new filmmaker, this book is perfect for you. You can browse through the pages in any order, discovering new cinematic techniques. You can use those techniques in your own films, watch the movies that are listed to see how the professionals use them, and grow as a filmmaker.

If you are a film buff, you'll find that this book is very easy to understand, even for those who don't know anything about the film industry. If you want to know more about how movies work, learn the techniques and watch for them in your favorite films. Learn to enjoy the moviegoing experience more fully by understanding how cinema really works.

If you are an experienced filmmaker, a storyboard artist, or an animator, use this book as a reference. It is the culmination of hundreds of hours of research. Why should you have to spend that amount of time when it's already been done for you?

Please enjoy.

CONTENTS

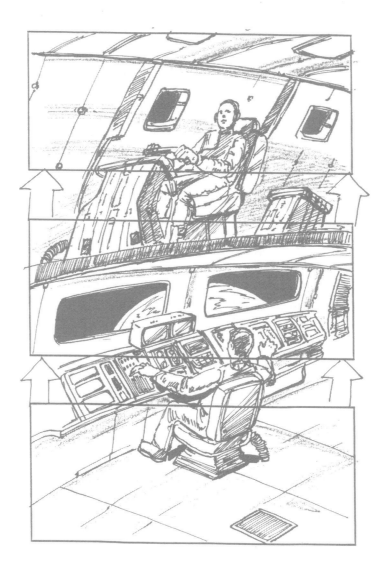

INTRODUCTION

This book began several years ago, when I became interested in how movies work. I started to re-view movie scenes in order to learn, jotting down cinematic techniques that I saw. Eventually, I began to recognize common techniques that were used in many different films. I continued to find and record cinematic techniques until that research formed the genesis of this book.

By reading this book, you will soon be able to identify many of the techniques used in films, commercials, and music videos. This knowledge is invaluable for film students, and should be helpful for anyone who wants to find out how movies "work." Of course there is no way that I could cover every possible filmmaking technique, so only some of the most common are included here.

Each cinematic technique has been given a unique name— a condensed version of the technique's purpose and description. The names are arbitrary— you can call them whatever you want. The advantage to a label is that it gives you a tool to identify techniques used in the films you watch. This skill will greatly enhance your ability to learn from other people's films.

I have listed example films for many of these techniques, as well as storyboards. The disadvantage of illustrations is that they cannot fully represent a cinematic technique. If you are interested in a particular technique, rent one of the example films and watch it. You may even find yourself watching films that wouldn't have interested you before.

Filmmaking is much more than a technical skill. It's about establishing relationships with the cast and crew, becoming a leader, and pursuing your vision. Technical knowledge alone won't guarantee that you'll become a great filmmaker, but it will help you become more fluent in the language of cinema.

x

BASIC CINEMATIC TECHNIQUES

I set out to write this book because I wanted to reach beyond the basic cinematic elements that most filmmaking books describe, such as pan, tilt, and dolly. One of the best ways to learn about these elements is to watch as many movies as you can. Unfortunately, most people don't have that kind of time. This book simplifies the process by compiling the most common and distinct filmmaking techniques taken from hundreds of films.

It can't hurt to go over the basics one more time before we get into the next "level" of cinematic techniques. I have provided methods for conceptualizing each technique— a way of visualizing what the technique actually looks like. Visualization skills allow you to look at the world around you in a new, cinematic context. This new sight is similar to what artists see when they start to recognize lines and colors in the world, allowing them to create abstract representations of reality.

PAN

What does it look like?

Pan is the horizontal axis of camera movement. When the camera pans, it turns left and right. To conceptualize a *Pan*, stare straight ahead and turn your head to the left and to the right.

Panning is commonly used to look across a very wide panorama that doesn't fit within the camera frame— a landscape, for example. This technique can be used within a scene to follow characters or vehicles as they move around. This is known as re-framing the shot.

Pan with vehicle

Pan

TILT

What does it look like?

Tilt is the vertical axis of camera movement. When the camera tilts, it pivots up and down. Tilting is commonly used to look over tall objects such as a cathedral or an office building.

To conceptualize a Tilt, stare straight ahead and pivot your head to look up and down. Like the Pan, this technique is used within a scene to follow characters in motion— known as re-framing the shot.

Tilt

DOLLY

What does it look like?

Dolly is a very natural technique— the camera simply moves horizontally through space. The energy of this technique is similar to a person walking or riding on a moving platform— a wheelchair, for example. To conceptualize a *Dolly*, turn your head toward what you are interested in. Then walk forward and watch the world go by. This is how a *Dolly* movement looks to an audience.

Dolly movements may or may not use an actual dolly. Generally some kind of platform with wheels, the dolly moves along tracks that deter-

Dolly

mine the direction of movement. Tracks must be used because pushing the platform over uneven ground results in shaky and erratic camera movement. The Steadicam™ is an alternative device that allows a camera to be carried, without experiencing the bumps and jiggles usually associated with handheld camera work. This makes the camera appear to be "floating" through the air. If a camera operator has a steady grip, handheld cameras can create dolly-like movements as well.

MECHANICAL

What does it look like?

Mechanical techniques include the use of devices that allow filmmakers to create unique and interesting camera movements. These are easier to conceptualize when we can move as the camera does— which is possible if a device has a platform that we can sit or stand on.

Cranes and Jibs are the most common examples of mechanical devices. Each of these devices has a mechanical "arm" on which the camera is mounted. This arm hinges on a pivot that frees the camera to move through space, allowing the creation of sweeping, dramatic camera movements.

There are many other specialized mechanical devices available. Each device creates a unique type of motion that alters the audience's perception of a film in some special way.

Crane Sequence

PULL FOCUS

What does it look like?

Pulling Focus is a considered a natural camera technique. Like our eyes, which pull focus whenever we look at objects that are at different distances in our field of vision, it changes our focus.

We can either be focused on something close up or on something far away. Since we don't have the ability to focus on both at the same time, our eyes must *Pull Focus* to compensate.

When making a film, *Pulling Focus* is often necessary because most camera lenses don't keep the entire scene in focus. As the camera moves around, a crew member called a "focus puller" will adjust the focus to match whatever the camera is looking at.

To conceptualize this technique, consciously focus on objects at different depths as you look around.

Pull Focus

ZOOM

What does it look like?

The focal length of a camera lens determines the distance that the camera can "see." Zoom lenses allow the focal length to be gradually changed. With a *Zoom*, the frame may transition from a wide shot to a close-up without ever moving the camera.

The *Zoom* is considered an unnatural technique because our eyes aren't able to incrementally change their focal length. Because of this, *Zooms* are often used for effect.

A very slow *Zoom* can be a subtle alternative to a dolly movement in locations where there is no room to rig a dolly and track. A very fast *Zoom*— a whip zoom— can be used to draw attention to objects in a scene.

Where can I see it?

The Color of Money uses both fast and slow zooms in many scenes. The Wild Bunch showcases many different kinds of zooms— slow, fast, short, extended, zoom in, and zoom out.

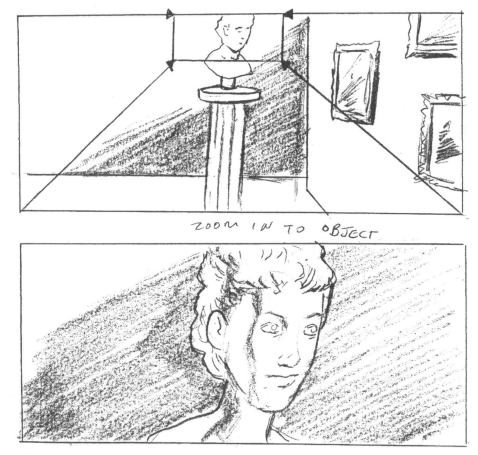

ZOOM IN TO OBJECT

Zoom

TRANSITION

What does it look like?

A *Transition* is any method for switching from one image to another.

The simplest of all *Transitions* is the cut. A cut may appear seamless to the audience, or it may be used to create harsh jumps in time and space.

Dissolves are very common in movies. A dissolve layers a new image over the old one, gradually increasing the new image's opacity until the transition is complete. Dissolves create a "soft" *Transition*.

Fades slowly change to an image from a colored screen or from an image to a color. The fade color is usually black, but not exclusively. For example: fading to white frequently shows some kind of "explosive" *Transition*. A fade to red could induce the imagery of blood; or blue of the ocean. Fades often begin and end scenes.

Effects *Transitions* use a special effect to transform one image into another. Examples of effects *Transitions* include wipes, page turns, vertical blinds, and morphing. Effects *Transitions* may be accomplished with specialized equipment such as an optical printer, or with a computer.

Where can I see it?

Effects *Transitions* give <u>Star Wars</u> the feel of an old science fiction B-movie. At the end of <u>Jacob's Ladder</u>, the scenery fades to white as Jacob ascends into heaven with his son.

MONTAGE

What does it look like?

What is *Montage*? There are at least a few recognizable definitions for the word. The most common of these is: a specific sequence of images in a film, usually without words and often set to music. For clarity I choose to call this the "Montage Sequence." Many films use this technique to express the passage of time or a sequence of events with little or no dialogue.

According to *Webster's Dictionary*, a montage is "the combination of elements of different pictures, esp. photographic." If we go by this definition, then a montage is simply a series of images— like the cuts in a film. Therefore, every film is an example of montage.

Perhaps the best description of montage can be found in the writings of Sergei Eisenstein, one of the forefathers of modern film theory. Eisenstein said that montage can be seen in films, and that its essence can be seen everywhere— in writing, in music, in art. Eisenstein's definition of montage allows for a broader definition— the collection of "elements" that build something— the tastes, sights, sounds, textures, and smells. Because film is purely an audio-visual medium, film montage is based on building up structures that affect the visual and audio senses.

Even though montage is a very important aspect of film, it can be detrimental if not used correctly. André Bazin, a respected French film critic, argued that the lack of montage can actually be beneficial for certain types of films. The reduction of splicing and cutting in a film gives the audience a more realistic perception of the story's time and space. Without montage, a director cannot cut away to hide falsehoods and mistakes.

FRAMING TERMS

Common terms used to frame objects within a scene are generally applied to actors, but can refer to inanimate objects as well. Examples are: a close-up of a phone or an extreme close-up of a coin slot. A director will often capture a collection of master shots, medium shots, and close-ups to provide a variety of footage during editing.

Master/Establishing Shot

Full Shot

Medium Shot

Medium Close-up

Close-up

Extreme Close-up

EXERCISES

• **Pick some of your favorite movies and watch them again.** Instead of watching them for the story, concentrate on the basic techniques the director uses, such as pan, tilt, dolly, mechanical, pull focus, and zoom.

• **Watch for different types of transitions.** Keep an eye out for cuts, fades, dissolves, and wipes. If you have the capability, slow the VCR to observe quick transitions in slow motion.

• **Learn about montage.** There are many good books on the subject, including the works of Sergei Eisenstein and André Bazin. Montage is a fundamental element of cinema. By exploring this technique, you'll greatly expand your knowledge and your ability to comprehend how films are made.

• **Seek out montage.** Not only will you see montage in movies, but you'll discover that it's a fundamental aspect of art, music, and other fields of creation. Observe how smaller components are combined to create the collection of elements that an audience enjoys.

• **Watch for close-ups, establishing shots, extreme close-ups.** Observe how the director changes the meaning of a shot by the way he frames actors or objects in a scene.

COMPOSITION TECHNIQUES

What is composition? Composition describes the way a director positions, groups, arranges, and views objects within the frame when he's filming a scene. Maybe he composes the shot so that the good characters are all on the left side of the screen and the evil characters are all on the right. Maybe he tilts the camera slightly to add tension to a scene.

The concept of composition is inherited from thousands of years of art history, and is every bit as meaningful in the world of motion pictures. This book is by no means meant to be an authoritative subject on framing and composition. There are plenty of good books already written on that subject. However, some of the composition techniques that are used most often in filmmaking are included here.

CAMERA HEIGHT

What does it look like?

The height of the camera has a considerable effect on the meaning of a shot.

If you only show a person's feet, there is a mystery— who are they? This is a very common technique. If you show their upper body but not their face, you discover more about them (they might be doing something with their hands), but you still don't really know who they are. Finally, when the camera is brought up to eye level with the actor, the mystery is resolved and the character is revealed.

Where can I see it?

Rosemary's Baby— near the end, in the scene where Rosemary is carrying a knife. The camera alternates *Camera Heights* to show different aspects of her emotional state. Her feet, the knife in her hands, and a close-up of her fear and anxiety all heighten the effect of the scene.

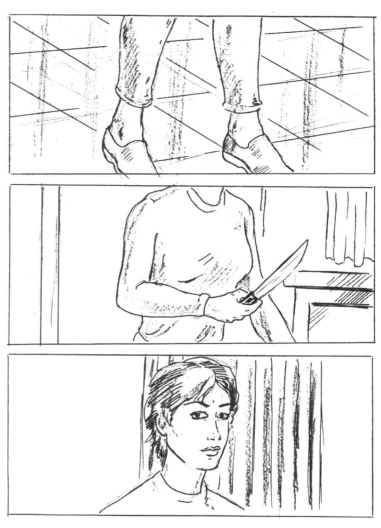

Camera Heights

DRAMATIC ANGLE, EXTREME ANGLE, BIRD'S-EYE VIEW

What does it look like?

A *Dramatic Angle* adds to the emotional impact of a scene. A low camera angle makes characters and objects seem tall and powerful. A high camera angle gives the characters a diminished feel— as if the audience is looking down on them.

An *Extreme Angle* is a magnified version of a *Dramatic Angle*. An extreme low angle might start below the feet of a subject, staring up into the sky. An extreme high angle could be the view from the top of a tall office building, looking down on the insignificance of humanity.

A *Bird's-Eye View* is an *Extreme Angle* in which the camera is positioned directly above a scene, facing straight down.

Where can I see it?

The Crow uses many *Extreme Angles* to achieve the aesthetic of a comic book, a medium which commonly exaggerates angles and perspective. In Terminator 2: Judgment Day, many of the sequences with the Terminator are shot from a low angle. This technique enhances his image of strength.

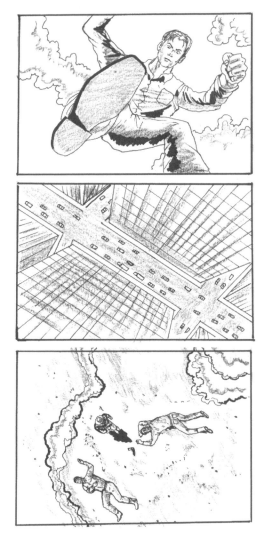

Dramatic Angles

SCREEN DIRECTION

What does it look like?

Essential to establishing the visual flow of a collection of shots, *Screen Direction* is simply the direction an object is facing in a scene— left or right. *Screen Direction* can maintain a visual continuity when making cuts, or it can be used in a non-standard way to add impact to a scene.

For example: If a director is filming two actors talking to each other, he might want to use close-ups. He must be careful to always film the actors from the same side. If he doesn't do this, one of the actors might face the right side of the screen in sections of the dialogue and the left side of the screen in others. This would be very disconcerting to an audience.

This is commonly referred to as the 180° rule— you must stay within a 180° arc of the actors in order to maintain consistent *Screen Direction*. Of course, all rules can be broken at the director's discretion.

Where can I see it?

In <u>Das Boot</u>, the submarine always faces toward the right side of the screen when traveling out to sea and toward the left when coming back to port.

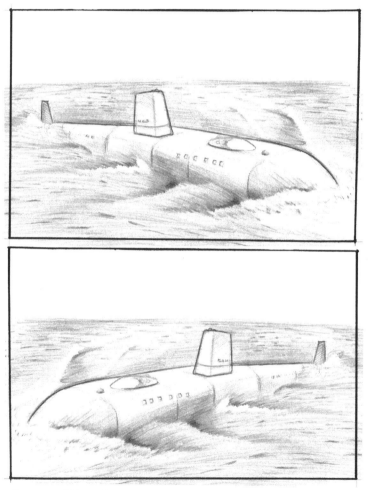

Screen Direction

TILTED HORIZON

What does it look like?

Tilted Horizon simply involves tipping the camera slightly to the side in order to increase the tension in a scene.

Also known as a Dutch angle or a canted shot, this technique is most effective when there are strong horizontal and vertical lines that the non-uniform camera angle enhances.

Because our eyes are used to seeing everything straight up and down, the diagonals that result from *Tilted Horizon* tend to attract our attention.

Where can I see it?

Tilted Horizon is used extensively throughout <u>The Third Man</u>.

Tilted Horizon

EXTREME CLOSE-UP

What does it look like?

An *Extreme Close-Up* is simply a magnified view of a small object, causing it to fill the entire frame.

Extreme Close-Ups are effective because we are not used to seeing an abnormally magnified level of detail. By filling the frame with a singular feature, the audience's attention is drawn to that subject, to the exclusion of everything else.

Extreme Close-Ups can be used to emphasize a particular scene or a sequence of dialogue. For example: if a character is nervous, the director might cut to an *Extreme Close-Up* of the actor wringing his hands or shifting her eyes.

Where can I see it?

In <u>U Turn</u>, *Extreme Close-Ups* are frequently cut in at odd intervals with the action and dialogue. In <u>The Fifth Element</u>, we see an *Extreme Close-Up* of Leeloo's eye opening as she discovers the horrors of war.

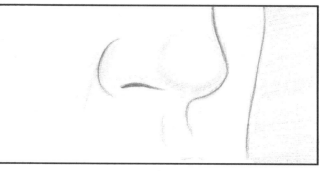
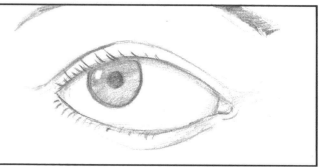

Extreme Close-Ups

STAGING

What does it look like?

Staging is somewhat the opposite of montage. Instead of cutting between wide shots, close-ups, reversals, and cutaways, *Staging* involves filming in very long sections.

Staging derives its name from its similarity to watching a play being performed on stage. When you watch a play, there is no camera to cut back and forth between the actors. The audience sees all of the action being performed from a single distance and angle.

Where can I see it?

<u>Rope</u> is an experimental Hitchcock film composed of extremely long takes. Woody Allen is known for filming scenes as very long sequences without cutting. This gives the actors more freedom to improvise, because they don't have to worry about how the editor will splice the cuts together in post-production.

Staging

DEPTH STAGING, PLANAR STAGING

What does it look like?

Throughout the history of film, different waves of film style have emphasized varying aspects of staging within the camera frame.

Depth Staging involves placing the characters in the frame at excessive distances from each other, emphasizing depth. One character could be all the way down the hallway, while the other character sits in close-up toward the front.

Planar Staging has roots in the theater, where all the characters are lined up on a stage. *Planar Staging* emphasizes a flat surface for staging a scene.

Where can I see it?

Citizen Kane makes considerable use of *Depth Staging*. In 2001: A Space Odyssey, there is a conference in which the speaker stands at a podium far in the background.

Planar Staging

Depth Staging

MULTI-LEVEL ACTION

What does it look like?

With *Multi-Level Action*, the audience watches one scene occur in the foreground while another occurs in the background.

This can be an exciting way to bring together storylines or to show the relationships between multiple story paths in a film.

Where can I see it?

In <u>Red</u>, the camera focuses on two levels of an exterior scene. In the foreground is a man's girl-friend, walking toward his apartment. In the background, a model runs outside to turn off her car alarm.

Multi-Level Action

EXERCISES

• **Read a few good books on composition.** You can find this information in books about photography, fine arts, graphic design, and more. Composition has been studied for thousands of years. There is plenty of material on the subject.

• **Visit an art gallery or read a photography book.** Try to identify the compositional techniques you have learned within a work of art. Use these techniques in any films you direct.

• **Watch some movies and concentrate on how the director composes objects in a scene.** Skilled directors will use every cinematic technique available to them, including composition.

• **Practice composition.** You don't need an expensive film camera to do this. You can practice with pencil and paper, or by simply observing the composition of objects in the world around you.

CRANE TECHNIQUES

Cranes and jibs are mechanical devices, commonly used in filmmaking (see the "Mechanical" technique for more information). These machines can range in size from something that fits in the back of a truck to cranes that tower high into the air. The largest cranes are used to create very wide, sweeping camera movements.

A crane movement often adds a certain dramatic impact to a scene. Because of its grand nature, a crane technique will always be noticed by an audience. When used in combination with a dolly movement or a camera technique, a crane movement can provide an effect even greater than the sum of its parts.

If we were to reduce crane movement to its basic forms, we might say that there are only two crane techniques: crane up and crane down. However, there are many factors involved with crane techniques that allow each of these simple movements to convey a wide variety of expressions and emotions to an audience.

CRANE UP, MOVE AWAY, CRANE DOWN, MOVE TOWARD

What does it look like?

With *Crane Up, Move Away*, the camera starts at "eye level" with a scene that contains moving objects. For example: an actor on horseback or in a vehicle. As the actor, or object, moves away from us into the background, the camera cranes up. This combination of movements intensifies the action.

Crane Down, Move Toward is just the opposite. The subject starts far away from the crane and moves toward the camera. As the object gets closer, the camera cranes down until its height is at ground level.

Crane Up, Move Away

Where can I see it?

Both of these techniques are evident in <u>Thelma and Louise</u> and <u>The Untouchables</u>. *Crane Up, Move Away* can be seen when Harry and Sally drive away from college in <u>When Harry Met Sally</u>, and when Matilda walks away from a gunfight at the end of <u>The Professional</u>.

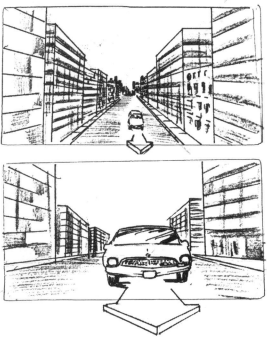

Crane Down, Move Toward

SEARCHING CRANE

What does it look like?

Searching Crane is a specialized crane technique. As a character onscreen searches for something, the camera slowly cranes upward, gradually revealing the magnitude of the search.

Where can I see it?

In <u>The Good, the Bad, and the Ugly</u>, the camera cranes back slightly to reveal the extent of a graveyard that must be searched to find the gold. In <u>House</u>, the camera cranes up from the pool as the main character searches for his son. <u>Labyrinth</u> uses a *Searching Crane* as Sarah searches through the labyrinth.

Searching Crane

RISE UP

What does it look like?

With *Rise Up*, the camera rises vertically. It rises toward something— a character's close-up, for example. *Rise Up* is often used to look over an obstruction— a railing or a fence— from the perspective of someone standing up.

Where can I see it?

At the end of <u>Batman</u>, the camera *Rises Up* through the city to reveal Batman standing at the top. At the end of <u>Batman Returns</u>, the camera *Rises Up* through the city superstructures to reveal Catwoman at the top. In <u>Desperado</u>, the camera *Rises Up* from the bar after El Mariachi reloads his gun in a shoot-out scene.

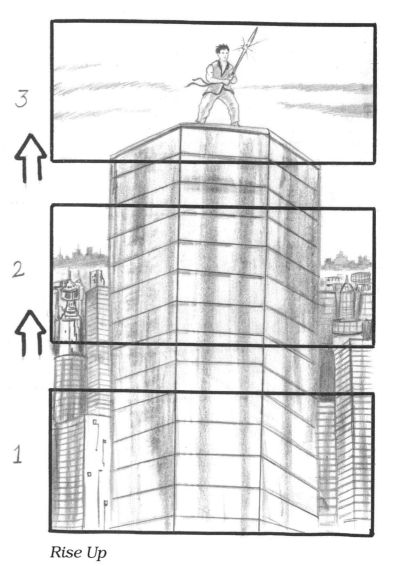

Rise Up

FALL DOWN

What does it look like?

Fall Down involves moving the camera vertically downward. Sometimes used to look at something on the ground by lowering the camera to ground level, *Fall Down* can also create a hiding effect. When the camera moves vertically behind an object, the effect is that the audience's perspective is hidden.

Where can I see it?

In <u>Red</u>, the camera *Falls Down* to reveal a man hiding, behind a lower wall, from his ex-girlfriend. The camera *Falls Down* through the city in <u>The Matrix</u>.

Fall Down

CRANE FRONT-TO-TOP

What does it look like?

For *Crane Front-To-Top*, the camera starts out directly in front of a character or an object. The camera begins to move forward and rises up at the same time, pivoting downward to keep the subject in frame. When the movement is finished, the camera sits directly above the subject, looking down from above.

Crane Front-To-Top is a nice dramatic movement that can add character to a scene.

Where can I see it?

Check out the meditation scene in <u>Hellraiser</u>. You can also see this in the temple scene at the beginning of <u>The Fifth Element</u>, where the focus of the camera movement is a statue of the perfect being.

Crane Front-To-Top

CRANE UP ENTRANCE

What does it look like?

Crane Up Entrance is often seen in explorer/adventure films, used when characters enter a town, village, or habitation. As the characters enter, the camera stops at the entrance and cranes upward. A view of the entire city is revealed to the audience as the camera rises. This can provide the audience with clues about what the characters will be facing on their journey.

Where can I see it?

In the beginning of <u>Greystoke: The Legend of Tarzan, Lord of the Apes</u>, *Crane Up Entrance* focus on a group of horse riders as they enter the Earl's courtyard. In <u>King Solomon's Mines</u>, *Crane Up Entrance* is used as the characters enter a village. In <u>Once Upon a Time in the West</u>, the camera cranes up from a train station to reveal a bustling western town.

Crane Up Entrance

CRANE UP EXPRESSION

What does it look like?

In addition to emphasizing depth, movement, and perspective, the camera can be moved in such a way that it invokes a purely emotional response.

Crane Up Expression works by craning the camera quickly upward during a time of a character's emotional distress.

This upward ascension can invoke a kind of psychological detachment or an expression of the grand nature of life.

Where can I see it?

In <u>The Crow</u>, *Crane Up Expression* is used as Eric Draven crawls out from his grave. In the 90's remake of <u>Great Expectations</u>, the camera cranes up quickly to express Finnegan's sorrow. In <u>Pleasantville</u>, the camera cranes up as Bud celebrates the newly born rain.

Crane Up Expression

CRANE UP, LOOK DOWN

What does it look like?

With *Crane Up, Look Down*, the camera rises above the subjects onscreen and tilts down.

The camera ends up looking down from a dramatic angle above. As an added benefit, this technique allows the audience to see what is on the ground below.

Where can I see it?

In <u>The Matrix</u>, *Crane Up, Look Down* shows us Neo standing on a skyscraper ledge. The camera cranes up to show how far the drop is to the ground below.

Crane Up, Look Down

CRANE DOWN, LOOK UP

What does it look like?

Crane Down, Look Up starts out with a level camera angle, facing the subject onscreen. The camera then moves down as it tilts up.

The scene transitions from a static angle to an exciting, dramatic angle from below.

Where can I see it?

In <u>Labyrinth</u>, *Crane Down, Look Up* is used when Sarah looks down over a precipice inside of the castle. In <u>Ed Wood</u>, the camera cranes down to look up at Bela Lugosi as he delivers a dramatic monologue. In <u>Jurassic Park</u>, the camera cranes down to look up at a cow being hoisted over the Raptor pen.

Crane Down, Look Up

EXERCISES

• **Visualize crane techniques.** You probably won't be able to get your hands on a crane, but you might be able to simulate the experience by finding a platform that moves in a similar way. Something as simple as a see-saw could be used to visualize small crane movements.

• **Read a book that talks about the mechanics of cranes, jibs, booms, and other equipment.** Learn what they look like so that you can identify them as you study filmmaking.

• **Watch for crane movements in films.** Observe how the director uses a simple crane up or crane down to express an idea, an emotion, or a plot point. Observe how the camera moves forward, tilts, or zooms during a crane movement for more variety.

TECHNIQUES OF MOVEMENT

This section contains a collection of techniques for moving the camera through space. A camera can be dollied. It can be flown through the air. It can be moved in combination with the movement of characters in a scene.

Movement of the camera or the lack thereof is essential to cinema. A moving camera alters an audience's perspective— making viewers feel as if they are taking a journey through the scene. A still camera allows the audience to focus on the dramatic rather than the cinematic aspects of a scene.

There are many devices that can move the camera. Each supplies its own unique kinetic energy to a moving camera technique. For those described as "dolly" techniques, the director doesn't have to use an actual dolly. He might use a Steadicam™, shoot the scene handheld, or place the camera in a moving vehicle.

CHARACTER DOLLY

What does it look like?

A *Character Dolly* is a forward camera movement that focuses on one or more characters in a scene. It is commonly noted in screenplays as "Push In."

The camera starts out with a wide shot of an actor and is pushed forward, reaching for the actor's close-up and beyond. This cinematic technique adds tension to the scene, acting like a magnifying glass on the character's emotional state. The actor doesn't have to be saying anything for the *Character Dolly* to be effective.

The speed of camera movement can greatly alter the emotional effect of this technique. A very slow *Character Dolly* will subtly highlight the scene's emotional qualities. More flamboyant films use a faster version for a comic or exciting effect.

Where can I see it?

Perhaps the most recognizable personification of the *Character Dolly* is in <u>The Godfather: Part II</u>. To end the film, Coppola simply moves the camera slowly towards a contemplative Michael Corleone, leaving the audience with a lasting impression of the character. Steven Spielberg uses this technique in many of his films.

Character Dolly

DISCOVERY

What does it look like?

A *Discovery* includes any shot that begins away from the action and then a camera movement that reveals a scene.

A common example of this technique occurs when the camera begins behind an obstacle that obscures an audience's view. The camera then moves out from behind that obstacle to discover the true subject of interest.

Another example of *Discovery* is a camera shot that starts out looking at nothing in particular; then, gradual movement reveals the action.

Where can I see it?

In <u>The Good, the Bad, and the Ugly</u>, the camera discovers Clint Eastwood by moving across the barrel of his rifle to his face. In <u>Four Weddings and a Funeral</u>, the camera reveals a bedroom and then moves to discover the lovers in bed. In <u>Goodfellas</u>, the camera swings around from the back of Ray Liotta's head to discover his face as he testifies in court.

Discovery

PULL BACK RETRACTION

What does it look like?

With *Pull Back Retraction*, the camera faces a scene and moves backwards.

The purpose of the camera movement is not to reveal anything new, but to distance the audience emotionally from the actions occurring onscreen.

Where can I see it?

Pull Back Retraction can be seen in <u>The Bride Wore Black</u>. The camera pulls back as one of Julie's victims suffocates in a storage compartment. As the camera pulls back, the trapped man's hopelessness is emphasized. At the end of <u>La Strada</u>, the camera pulls back from the Strong Man crying at the beach. This allows us to distance ourselves gradually from the character, allowing the film to end. This technique is similar to slowly turning down the volume to end a song.

In <u>The Graduate</u>, the camera pulls back from Ben at the bottom of the swimming pool as he contemplates his future. At the end of <u>Poltergeist</u>, the camera slowly pulls back from the television set that has been left outside.

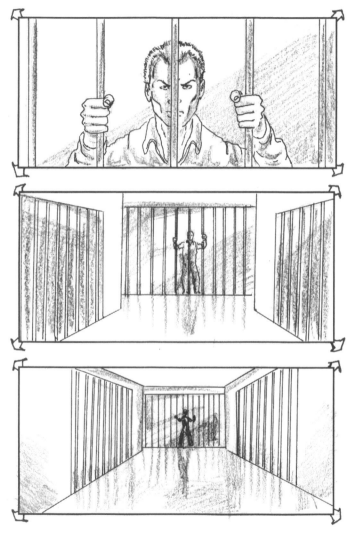

Pull Back Retraction

PULL BACK REVEAL

What does it look like?

With *Pull Back Reveal*, the camera moves backwards to reveal the true extent of a scene.

This technique gradually expands our understanding of a character's surroundings by revealing more of the character's world as the camera moves farther away.

Where can I see it?

In <u>Goodfellas</u>, the camera pulls back from a cross on Ray Liotta's neck as he arrives for a date. In <u>Cinema Paradiso</u>, the camera pulls back from a burned out movie theater to reveal the crowd looking on.

In <u>The Exorcist</u>, the camera pulls back from a mother yelling on the phone to reveal her daughter listening in the hallway. At the end of <u>Citizen Kane</u>, the camera pulls back to reveal the vast amount of possessions that Kane collected over the years.

Pull Back Reveal

SPIN AROUND

What does it look like?

Spin Around involves circling the camera around the scene in progress, creating a dizzying kinetic effect. You might also hear this referred to as a "360° Dolly."

Spin Around is simple, and it adds positive motion and energy to a scene. The camera doesn't have to move very fast for this to be effective.

Where can I see it?

In <u>The Untouchables</u>, the camera *Spins Around* the characters at dinner after their first successful raid. In <u>The Color of Money</u>, the camera *Spins Around* the pool table as the characters compete.

In <u>The Matrix</u>, the camera *Spins Around* a telephone as the characters are transported into their virtual existence. You can also see this in <u>The Crow</u>, when Sarah talks to Eric in his apartment after he's been resurrected.

Spin Around

FLY OVER

What does it look like?

Fly Over is a technique in which the camera is carried in a flying aircraft—an airplane, a helicopter, a blimp, or a balloon.

Fly Over is a grand way to show entire landscapes, covering more area, with more maneuverability than that of any ground-based camera. This technique is commonly used for establishing shots, to begin and end films, and to follow moving objects from far above.

When *Fly Over* is used over large cities, the camera often points straight down. This emphasizes the heightA of the buildings below.

Fly Over

Where can I see it?

In <u>The Shining</u>, you can see a helicopter's shadow on the hillside as *Fly Over* is used to follow Jack's car driving along the road. In <u>Scream 2</u>, the camera flies up from ground level to the sky to end the film. In <u>The Replacement Killers</u>, the camera flies over the city. *Fly Over* is used extensively in <u>Braveheart</u>.

DEPTH DOLLY

What does it look like?

A *Depth Dolly* is a camera movement that is perpendicular to a scene's line of action, increasing the sense of depth.

Characters move toward the camera and away from the camera. To further emphasize depth, the camera will occasionally move in front of objects that temporarily obscure the camera's view. These foreground objects contrast with objects far in the background.

Where can I see it?

Depth Dolly can be seen as the students run across campus in <u>Good Will Hunting</u>.

Depth Dolly

DOLLY UP,
DOLLY DOWN

What does it look like?

When a camera is moved around, the angle of the camera makes an impact on the meaning of the shot. Most dollies are fairly level as they follow the characters onscreen.

Dolly Up and *Dolly Down* are specialized techniques. When the camera is moved, it's tilted unusually high or low. *Dolly Up* emphasizes the height and vastness of a character's surroundings. *Dolly Down* can transform the ground rolling by into a cinematic event.

Where can I see it?

At the beginning of <u>La Femme Nikita</u>, *Dolly Down* is used as the camera traverses the streets of France. At the end of <u>Terminator 2: Judgment Day</u>, *Dolly Down* shows the seemingly endless highway flowing by. Near the beginning of <u>Rashomon</u>, *Dolly Up* looks up toward the trees as the woodsman walks through the forest.

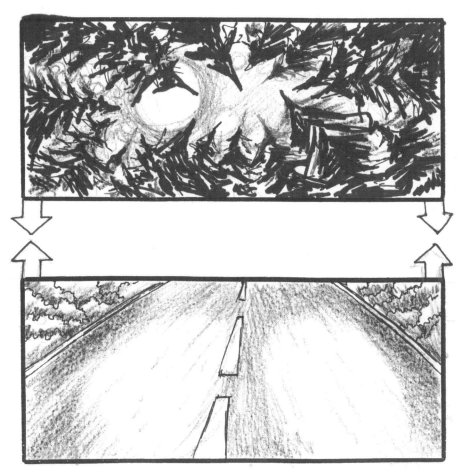

Dolly Up, Dolly Down

SPIN LOOK

What does it look like?

With *Spin Look*, the camera spins around an actor to get a glimpse of what he is looking at. The camera may also begin by viewing the object, then spin back around to view the character.

Spin Look is an alternative to the popular technique of cutting away when a character looks offscreen.

Where can I see it?

In <u>Tombstone</u>, the camera spins around Wyatt Earp as he looks toward a group of horses approaching. *Spin Look* is used several times in <u>After Hours</u>, as Paul explores New York City at night.

Spin Look

TRACK THROUGH SOLID

What does it look like?

A filmmaker can use *Track Through Solid* to give the appearance of tracking through a solid object.

To create this effect, an object is cut open so that the camera can pan, tilt, or move in front of the cutaway portion. When this technique is used, it seems as if the camera has accomplished something impossible, but it is actually a rather straightforward visual trick.

Where can I see it?

Watch <u>Blade Runner</u>. When Deckard enters the building, the camera cranes down "through" the roof of the police office. What actually happens is that the office is a cutaway set, and the camera cranes down in front of it. Most audiences will never notice this strange transition. You can also see this technique in <u>Bound</u>, when the camera moves over a wall that divides the two apartments.

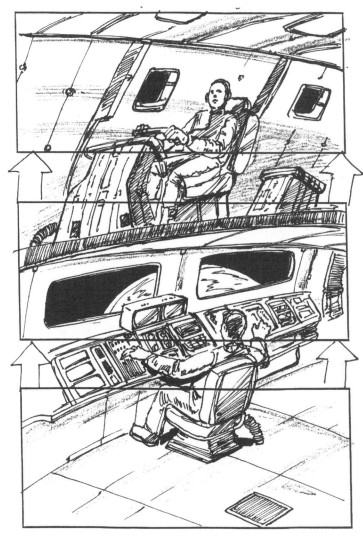

Track Through Solid

VERTIGO

What does it look like?

Commonly referred to as a "Dolly Zoom," *Vertigo* exaggerates perspective, but keeps objects in the center of the frame at the same apparent size. This is achieved by moving the camera forward while zooming out at the same time, or by moving the camera back and zooming in.

This technique is used to create the effects of dizziness, confusion, ecstasy, boredom, or surprise.

Where can I see it?

Watch Alfred Hitchcock's <u>Vertigo</u>, in the end where James Stewart tries desperately to conquer his fear of heights. In <u>Jaws</u>, when Martin Brody sees the shark attack at the beach. In <u>The Mask</u>, Cameron Diaz's sexy character steps into the room, and Jim Carrey and his co-star suffer the effects of *Vertigo*.

A very slow *Vertigo* is used near the end of <u>Goodfellas</u>, when Ray Liotta and Robert DeNiro sit across from each other in the diner.

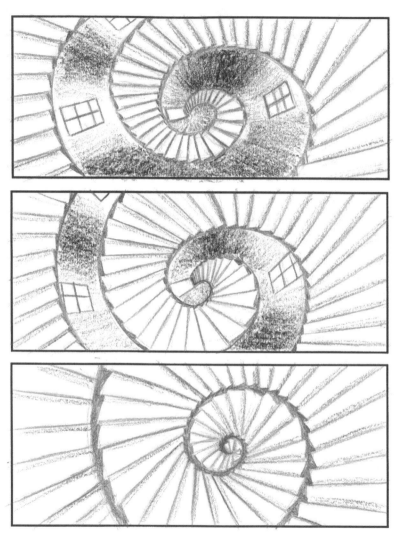

Vertigo

EXPAND DOLLY

What does it look like?

With *Expand Dolly*, the camera follows an actor who is moving away. As the camera moves forward, the actor walks faster than the camera— distancing himself from the audience.

Expand Dolly adds finality to a scene, and is a nice setup for a transition or a fade.

Expand Dolly

CONTRACT DOLLY

What does it look like?

A *Contract Dolly* moves the camera forward as an actor walks toward the camera at the same time, making a simple action more dramatic. Combining two opposite actions increases the intensity of the character's forward movement.

If the camera can't be moved, an equally dramatic effect can be achieved when the actor walks toward the camera, and the camera tilts up to keep the actor's close-up in frame.

Where can I see it?

Contract Dolly is used during an airport chase scene in <u>Face/Off</u>. In <u>Raiders of the Lost Ark</u>, a distraught Indiana Jones runs up to the camera, demonstrating a modified version of this technique.

Contract Dolly

COLLAPSE DOLLY

What does it look like?

Collapse Dolly starts out with the camera moving backwards while facing an actor. The actor walks faster than the camera, eventually overtaking it. The actor then passes out of frame to the left or right.

Collapse Dolly is a good technique for adding finality to a scene.

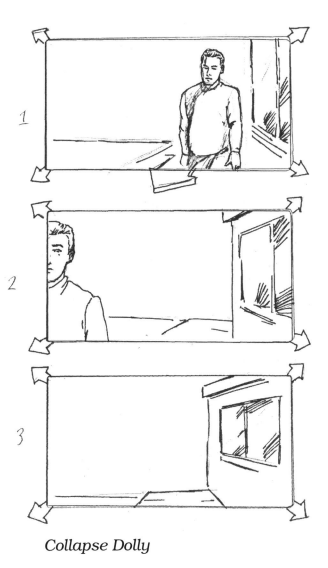

Collapse Dolly

EXERCISES

• **Try to think of unique ways to move the camera.** Examples: merry-go-rounds, swings, inside a car, on a roller coaster, walking along, on top of a skateboard, on a bike, lowered to the ground, or dancing. Each and every one of these movements can add its own unique kinetic energy to a scene.

• **Build your own dolly.** It can be as simple as a board with wheels. You might use something that you already have: a wheelchair, a stroller, a bicycle. Or, simply walk along to visualize dolly movements as you look around.

• **Practice combining movements.** Examples: camera moves forward and actors move toward the camera; camera moves backward and actors move past the camera; camera moves sideways and actors move away from the camera. Learn how different combinations of movement can be used to affect the audience.

• **Practice the Track Through Solid technique.** You might do this by using a table that can be split into halves, or a thin wall that divides two separate scenes.

TECHNIQUES OF PERSPECTIVE

Perspective is all about how we look at things. A skilled filmmaker can manipulate an audience's perspective, even draw us into the subjective experience of a character onscreen. Movies are allowed to distort our perspective, and we welcome it.

Directors have a variety of cinematic techniques at their disposal for molding the perspective of a scene. By skillfully blending a well known photographic image with a manipulated form of imagery, the director can communicate new ideas in film. A number of these cinematic techniques are discussed here.

POV

What does it look like?

POV stands for "point of view," meaning that the audience sees exactly what a character in a film sees.

POV can be used to increase the audience's emotional attachment to the characters onscreen.

Where can I see it?

In <u>Jaws</u> there are sequences projected from the shark's *POV*. <u>Terminator 2: Judgment Day</u> shows a computerized *POV* when looking through the eyes of the Terminator. In <u>Natural Born Killers</u>, a very intense *POV* is achieved by assuming the perspective of Mallory when she slams her head against the prison walls.

POV

Strange Days uses many *POV* shots in its virtual reality sequences. The <u>Evil Dead</u> series uses *POV* to show the movement of an evil presence through the woods. In <u>The Exorcist</u>, we see Father Karras' *POV* when he falls down the stairs.

INVENTORY POV

What does it look like?

Inventory POV is a variation on the standard POV technique. The character carries an object in front of his face— a knife or a gun for example. This object shows up in the frame and allows the audience to see what he is holding in his hands.

Where can I see it?

Inventory POV is used in <u>Evil Dead 2</u>, <u>La Femme Nikita</u>, and <u>The Fifth Element</u>, as characters wield weapons during action sequences. At the end of <u>Spellbound</u>, we see an Inventory POV as the doctor points his revolver and turns it to kill himself.

Inventory POV

POV OBJECT,
POV PROJECTILE

What does it look like?

POV Object takes the perspective of an inanimate object—an answering machine or a soda can for example. When an actor reaches toward that object or interacts with it, the audience sees the scene from a unique perspective.

POV Projectile follows a projectile such as a bullet or an arrow to its destination. This allows the audience to "experience" the projectile and its effects.

Where can I see it?

In <u>After Hours</u>, the camera takes the POV of a key ring that's thrown out the window. <u>Robin Hood: Prince of Thieves</u> and <u>Army of Darkness</u> both use the *POV Projectile* technique to show an arrow flying through the air toward its target.

<u>La Femme Nikita</u> takes the perspective of a bullet flying toward its victim during a kitchen gunfight. <u>The Color of Money</u> gives us the perspective of a pool ball traveling across a table.

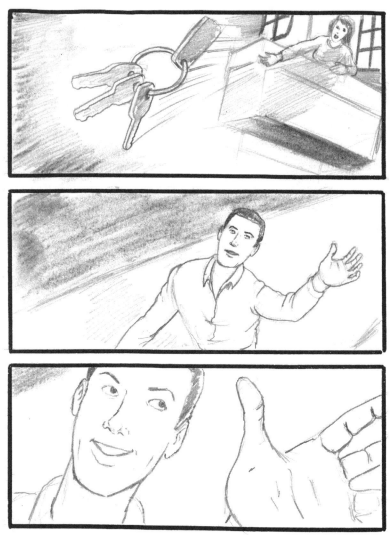

POV Object

VOYEUR

What does it look like?

In a sense we are all voyeurs— spying on the private and intimate lives of the characters onscreen. Those characters don't ask us to intrude into their existence. We simply oblige ourselves, and gouge our appetite for realities other than our own.

A voyeuristic sequence may be specifically designed to make us feel that we are spying on the characters onscreen, rather than simply experiencing the story being told. A shot may be framed in such a way (through binoculars, from inside a closet) that emphasizes the voyeuristic aspect of the scene.

Voyeur

Where can I see it?

Many detective movies, including <u>Rear Window</u> and <u>Blue Velvet</u>, contain elements of voyeurism. The detective spends his time spying into other peoples' lives. The voyeuristic element can be subtle, or it can be very direct. In <u>She's Gotta Have It</u>, <u>Goodfellas</u>, <u>Ferris Bueller's Day Off</u>, and <u>Cadillac Man</u>, the characters temporarily break out of their reality and talk directly to the audience through the camera. This has a somewhat jolting effect in <u>Goodfellas</u>, when Ray Liotta's character explains himself in the courtroom.

DARK VOYEUR

What does it look like?

Dark Voyeur is the classic horror and psychological thriller gimmick. The technique is used to evoke feelings of the characters in a film being watched, usually by someone or something with malicious intentions.

This technique works by framing the characters in the scene *through* the bushes or *from inside* the closet. This gives the impression that someone is watching them, but doesn't want to be seen.

Where can I see it?

<u>Friday the 13th</u> is a good film to watch for the *Dark Voyeur*. We get the shark's perspective in <u>Jaws</u>, as it looks up at the swimmers. Many horror films use this technique.

Dark Voyeur

MASK, VIGNETTE

What does it look like?

A *Mask* is an area of the screen that is blacked out to represent what we would see if our field of vision was reduced. Examples of *Masks* can be seen in films where a character looks through an object such as a pair of binoculars or a keyhole.

A *Vignette* is similar to a *Mask*. The difference is that a *Mask* is always a blacked-out area. A *Vignette*, on the other hand, may have some shape or form. For example, looking through a hidden camera might show the rounded edges of the camera lens surrounding the screen. Because the masked area has color and form, we refer to it as a *Vignette*.

Where can I see it?

In <u>Das Boot</u>, a *Mask* shows the submarine captain looking through binoculars at a destroyer. <u>The Truman Show</u> contains many *Vignettes*. Each one represents a hidden camera in Truman's world.

Mask, Vignette

REFLECTION

What does it look like?

A *Reflection* is enigmatic and philosophically interesting. Instead of seeing the world as it really is, we see a reflected image. This forces us to see a reality that has been distorted for a brief period of time.

There are many different ways that we can see reflections. Mirrors and other reflective objects are common examples.

Where can I see it?

In <u>Jurassic Park</u>, we see the T-Rex's *Reflection* in the jeep's rear view mirror as the characters speed away. In <u>Blue</u>, the image of a doctor is reflected in Julie's eyes, as he tells her that her husband and daughter have died. In <u>Duel</u>, *Reflections* in car mirrors represent the film's road-centric theme.

Reflection

PORTAL

What does it look like?

A *Portal* is a way of looking at reality as it is filtered through some kind of device.

Looking at a television set is seeing reality, but what you are seeing is not physically real. It is merely an imported representation of someone else's perception— a *Portal* into another person's existence.

Where can I see it?

In <u>Numero Deux</u>, Godard shows the entire film through two television sets which act as *Portals* into the characters' lives. In <u>Blue</u>, Julie views her family's funeral through a small video monitor from her hospital bed. In <u>The Truman Show</u>, Truman's entire life is viewed through hundreds of hidden cameras. Each camera is a *Portal* into his life.

Portals

SHADOW

What does it look like?

A unique representation of reality, a *Shadow* can help a filmmaker who wants to show a scene's action indirectly.

Shadows are useful when it is difficult or undesirable to show what is actually taking place in a scene. For example, instead of showing us a character being beheaded, the director shows us a shadow that represents this action.

Shadows may also be used to "soften" a film's rating, by only indirectly showing something that, if projected explicitly, would cause concern.

Where can I see it?

Shadow

In <u>Evil Dead 2</u>, we see Ash's *Shadow* as he decapitates a possessed corpse with a chainsaw. In <u>M</u>, a *Shadow* shows a child killer approaching his newest victim. In <u>The Good, the Bad, and the Ugly</u>, a *Shadow* is used as Clint Eastwood arrives in the graveyard.

SILHOUETTE

What does it look like?

A *Silhouette* is created by placing film characters against very strong backlighting so that the characters' features and expressions become darkened or even completely black.

This technique can be used to contrast a character with his surroundings— a man silhouetted against a blazing sunset for example. *Silhouettes* are often used for artistic expression.

Where can I see it?

In Full Metal Jacket, we see the *Silhouettes* of soldiers as they train in boot camp. We see this in Unforgiven, when Clint Eastwood rides on horseback across the plains. In Jaws, Roy Scheider's body is photographed as a *Sillhouette* on the fishing boat at night. In Kickboxer, we see a *Silhouette* of Van Damme as he trains in the temple ruins.

Silhouette

SUBJECTIVE

What does it look like?

The *Subjective* technique involves strapping or connecting a camera to an actor's body. When this is done, the camera becomes a part of that character's subjective experience. When the character moves, the camera moves with him. The camera usually faces the character's close-up to connect even further.

Where can I see it?

In <u>Mean Streets</u>, the camera is strapped to Harvey Keitel, following him as he stumbles through a party. In <u>The Exorcist</u>, the camera is strapped to a psychiatrist and we fall backward with him after Regan attacks.

In <u>Strictly Ballroom</u>, Scott Hastings stands on a platform that spins around as he spins. The camera moves on the platform, inside his subjective reality. In <u>Jacob's Ladder</u>, *Subjective* is used to intensify Jacob's nightmarish experiences.

Subjective

EXERCISES

• **Look at the world around you and observe how reality is constantly being presented indirectly.** Examples: reflections, portals, and shadows. What's the difference between these examples and the reality we see with our own eyes?

• **Watch some horror films.** Why do you think Dark Voyeur is used so frequently, and why is such a simple technique so effective?

• **Create your own masks and vignettes.** You can cut a form out of cardboard and use it to frame a photograph, or you might draw a border around a magazine illustration.

• **Make a film that takes the perspective of some inanimate object.** You may be able to achieve some interesting scenarios with this technique.

• **Observe.** How do directors use the Subjective, POV, and Voyeur techniques to transport us into the internal perspective of a character onscreen?

CAMERA TECHNIQUES

This category includes cinematic techniques that are achieved by dealing with the camera itself, rather than with a device that moves the camera through space, such as a dolly or crane. Many of these techniques could conceivably be achieved by a single camera operator. Some of them might require special equipment to get the full effect.

Typically, a film camera has controls for exposure, focus, and focal length (zoom lenses). In addition to these controls, the camera can be panned, rotated, or flipped over. By manipulating the camera controls, and by manipulating the camera itself, the fragments of a cinematic language are revealed.

WHIP PAN, WHIP CUT

What does it look like?

With a *Whip Pan*, the camera is moved quickly from one angle to another, causing the image to blur from the motion. If the camera zooms in, the effect of the *Whip Pan* will increase. This is because more apparent distance is covered by the zoomed camera movement. *Whip Pan* is often accompanied by a swishing sound that emphasizes the effect.

The blur that occurs during a *Whip Pan* can be used to make a creative *Whip Cut*. By starting out with a *Whip Pan* and cutting to another *Whip Pan*, the audience never notices the difference between the two blurs, making for a transparent transition.

Where can I see it?

Whip Cuts are used in <u>Some Like it Hot</u>. *Whip Pans* and *Whip Cuts* are used frequently in <u>Breaking the Waves</u>. Towards the end of <u>Casino</u>, *Whip Pans* express the escalating intensity of the story.

Whip Pan

WHIP ZOOM LOOK

What does it look like?

Whip Zoom Look is created by zooming quickly toward an object.

Because zooming is an unnatural technique, whip zooms force our attention to a specific object or character in a scene.

Where can I see it?

In <u>Army of Darkness</u>— when Ash forges his new arm— the camera whip zooms towards each step in the process. In <u>The 'Burbs</u>, the camera whip zooms when skeletons are discovered in the trunk of the Klopeks' car. <u>The Quick and the Dead</u> uses this technique during a quick draw competition.

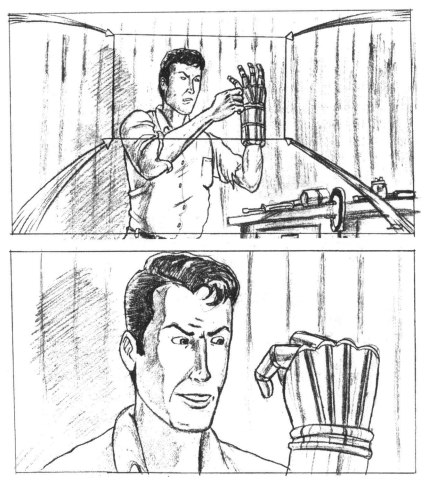

Whip Zoom Look

SEARCH UP

What does it look like?

Search Up is a technique used to gradually "describe" a character or an object. The camera moves slowly over an actor's body, gradually revealing information about the character. Finally, the camera ends up at the character's face, revealing her identity. This technique works with inanimate objects as well.

Where can I see it?

In the beginning of <u>Aliens</u>, the camera searches across Ripley's body: from a cigarette clasped in her hand to her close-up. In <u>Ace Ventura: Pet Detective</u>, *Search Up* is used when Lois Einhorn steps into the room. In <u>Terminator 2: Judgment Day</u>, the camera *Searches Up* from the Terminator's boots to his face as he steps out of the bar. In <u>Goodfellas</u>, the camera *Searches Up* Ray Liotta at the airport. In <u>Twins</u>, the camera uses *Search Up* as Arnold gets into the car with a beautiful blonde. In <u>The Bride Wore Black</u>, *Search Up* is used to show Julie in a white dress. In <u>Once Upon a Time in the West</u>, the camera *Searches Up* a lone gunman as he steps into the room. In <u>Easy Rider</u>, the camera searches across the characters' motorcycles.

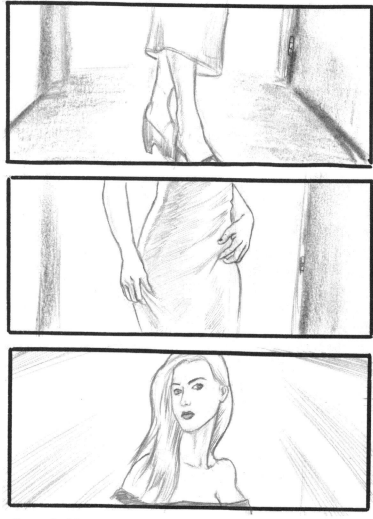

Search Up

BACK TO FRONT

What does it look like?

With *Back To Front*, we first see an action occur far in the background. As soon as that short scene is finished, the camera pulls focus and another scene occurs much closer to the camera.

Back To Front emphasizes depth, and is also used to compare and contrast two separate but related scenes without moving the camera.

Where can I see it?

Back To Front is used in <u>Terminator 2: Judgment Day</u>. First, Edward Furlong drives his motorcycle far in the background. Then the Terminator drives his motorcycle into frame very close to the camera. In <u>Cinema Paradiso</u>, the camera first looks down at the village square. Finally, a man's watch is pulled into frame.

Rack Focus

Back To Front

FOCUS OUT, PASS OUT

What does it look like?

Focus Out, Pass Out is a POV shot. The audience sees the world gradually losing focus as the character loses consciousness.

Focus Out, Pass Out is often used when a character has been knocked out cold, is falling asleep, or has been drugged.

Where can I see it?

Focus Out, Pass Out can be seen in <u>Point Break</u>, after Johnny Utah is knocked over the head during an attempted robbery. A modified version of this technique can be seen in <u>The Living Daylights</u>. When James Bond is drugged, we see his out-of-focus POV.

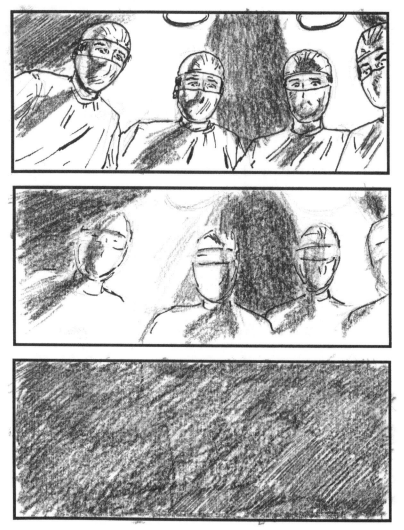

Focus Out, Pass Out

FOCUS TRANSITION

What does it look like?

Focus Transition is a specific type of transition achieved by changing the focus over time. This is similar to changing an image's brightness over time to accomplish a fade to black.

This out-of-focus technique sometimes starts a new scene. The image will be very blurry. As the camera focuses in, the scene is revealed.

Another version focuses out to prepare for the end of a scene. Or, these two techniques may be combined. First, the current scene is focused out and then the film cuts to a new scene that is out of focus. Finally, the new scene gains focus. Because the images are blurred, this technique can be used to make subtle cuts between scenes.

Where can I see it?

In <u>Batman</u>, the camera focuses in to a gambling scene. In <u>Once Upon a Time in the West</u>, the camera focuses in to a train arriving at the station.

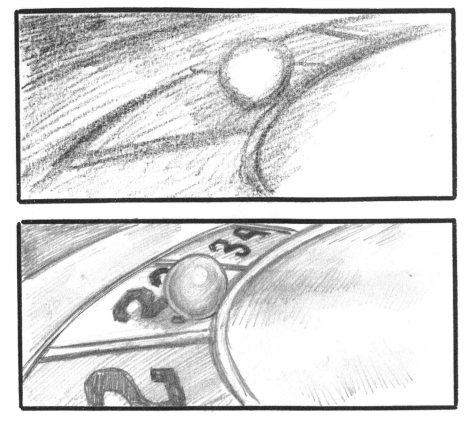

Focus Transition

OVEREXPOSE FADE, UNDEREXPOSE FADE

What does it look like?

These are two experimental techniques in which the exposure is changed gradually over time. The exposure controls the brightness of the film image. When an image is overexposed, it looks washed out. When an image is underexposed, it's difficult to make out details because of the dark image.

Overexpose Fade gradually overexposes the picture. This technique has been used to give a sense of enlightenment, or that something significant is beginning to change.

Underexpose Fade gradually underexposes the image. It can create a sense of foreboding or gloom.

Where can I see it?

You can see both *Overexpose Fade* and *Underexpose Fade* in <u>Wall Street</u>.

Underexpose Fade

Overexpose Fade

CEILING TWIST

What does it look like?

A *Ceiling Twist* is achieved by rotating the camera whenever it's pointed up toward something of interest. This object is often a ceiling of some sort. The camera may also move toward the object or away from it to add yet another dimension of movement.

A view of a ceiling by itself can be somewhat static and boring. A *Ceiling Twist* makes the simple act of looking up at something more interesting. The rotational energy transforms the shot.

Where can I see it?

At the end of Coppola's version of <u>Dracula</u>, the camera pulls down from a painted ceiling and rotates. At the end of <u>Titanic</u>, the camera looks up at the domed glass ceiling and rotates. In <u>Easy Rider</u>, the camera looks up at a painted ceiling and rotates.

Ceiling Twist

FLIP OVER

What does it look like?

Not only can the camera be tilted, panned, craned, dollied, and spinned, but it can flip over as well. *Flip Over* starts out looking at the world and ends up looking at the world upside down. Or vice versa.

Where can I see it?

In <u>The Tin Drum</u>, the camera *Flips Over* at Oskar's birth and *Flips Over* again after his father's death. In <u>2001: A Space Odyssey</u>, *Flip Over* emphasizes the lack of a horizon in space. The camera starts out upside down, looking at a space stewardess on the "ceiling." Finally it *Flips Over*.

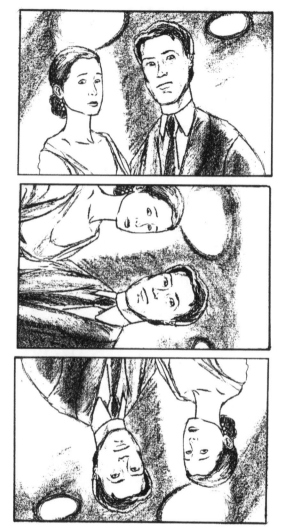

Flip Over

SHIFTING ANGLE

What does it look like?

A *Shifting Angle* is related to the Tilted Horizon technique. For a Tilted Horizon, the camera always stays tilted at the same angle. For a *Shifting Angle*, the camera continuously changes the viewing angle, inducing a dizzying effect. The camera continues to move and tilt back and forth.

Where can I see it?

The use of *Shifting Angles* in <u>Natural Born Killers</u> adds an incredible kinetic energy to the film. This technique may make you sick if you are prone to dizziness. Near the end of the original <u>Dangerous Liaisons</u>, the camera shifts from a static angle to a tilted angle when pushing in to a female lover's close-up. You can also experience this technique several times in <u>Raising Cain</u>.

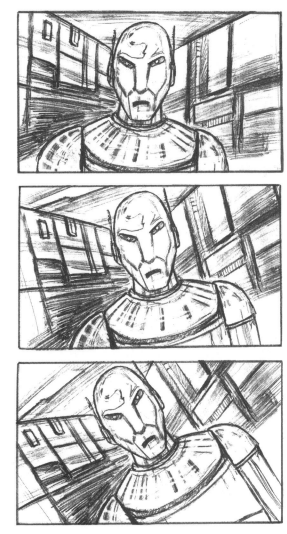

Shifting Angles

SLEEPOVER

What does it look like?

For a *Sleepover*, the camera is positioned directly above an actor, looking down from a bird's eye view. The camera rotates slowly, and may also rise or fall as it rotates to set up for a transition or a fade to black.

Sleepover is often employed when a character is asleep, unconscious, or lying down.

Where can I see it?

Watch <u>Four Rooms</u>— when the bellhop is knocked unconscious, *Sleepover* is used. Notice in <u>Batman</u>, when the camera looks down at the Joker's dead body from above. Towards the end of <u>Titanic</u>, the camera looks over Rose's body on a raft and spins slowly above her.

Sleepover

EXERCISES

• **Experiment with a camcorder or video camera.** See what effects you can achieve by tilting the camera, rotating it, and flipping it over. If you don't own a camera, you can cut a viewfinder out of cardboard and use it to visualize the techniques.

• **Use the Search Up technique to "describe" objects in your scenes.** Search across an object in different ways: top to bottom, left to right. How do the origin and end of the search affect the audience? If you start at the face of an actress and search down to her feet, the audience will get a different feeling than if you start at the feet of the actress and search up.

• **Try moving the camera quickly so that the image becomes blurred.** Experiment with different zoom distances to modify the effect.

• **Use out-of-focus, overexposed, or underexposed images to your advantage.** Learn how these flaws can be used to enhance the emotional quality of a scene.

EDITING TECHNIQUES

After a film is finished shooting, the production wraps and the film goes into post-production. During this period, film editors take all the footage shot by the director, over the course of weeks or months, and splice it together to make a movie. In addition, music, sound effects, and other extras are added to the final print.

Editing is the essence of montage. Without editing, a film would be more like a long documentary than a cinematic experience. Editing controls the rhythm of a scene— the beat. A skilled editor is able to make something beautiful out of a stack of footage reels.

Film editors have a wide array of tools at their disposal. They can edit films digitally in a non-linear editing system. They have tools to manipulate the color of the image, and to add dissolves, fades, titles, and transitions. They can work with specialized companies that create digital effects to augment reality. There are a number of cinematic techniques that are commonly used during the editing process.

JUMP CUT

What does it look like?

In most films, directors and editors do their best to hide cuts from us. They cut when an action occurs, cut when a character's eyes move, and use cutaways (see the Cutaway technique). Another technique is to make sure the angle and distance change significantly for each cut. This keeps the audience from noticing "jitters" in the scene.

Directors don't have to make a cut transparent; they can use a *Jump Cut*— any cut that isn't seamless. For example, if a character in a scene suddenly jumps from one part of the screen to the other without moving there, the audience will take notice to this *Jump Cut*.

Where can I see it?

In <u>Breaking the Waves</u>, many subtle jumps in space and time are used as *Jump Cuts*. In Godard's <u>Breathless</u>, jumps in time and space are made during the dialogue.

Jump Cuts

MATCH CUT

What does it look like?

A *Match Cut* is the antithesis of a jump cut. Instead of making us sit up and take notice when a cut occurs, *Match Cut* is used to make the transition from one image to another as seamless as possible.

The most common way to do this is to cut on the action. When an action is started in one frame, the camera cuts, and then the action is finished in the second frame. Because the audience is paying more attention to the action then they are to the cutting of the film, this cut can become almost transparent.

Another way to do this is to cut on a look. When an actor shifts his eyes to look at something, the camera cuts to a new image. This is a very natural transition because we experience the scene through the character's eyes. It is natural for us to see something new as the character looks around.

A *Match Cut* can be improved by changing the distance and angle for each cut to avoid "jitters" in a scene.

Match Cut

SUBLIMINAL CUT

What does it look like?

A *Subliminal Cut* is a cut that happens very quickly. The film cuts from the first image to a new, impact image, and then cuts back again. The new image lasts only a few frames, and the audience gets only a very brief glimpse of it.

This technique works like a subliminal message, activating something in the viewer's subconscious, but not necessarily registering at a conscious level.

Where can I see it?

In <u>The Exorcist</u>, Father Karras sees the face of death as a *Subliminal Cut* after his mother's death. In <u>From Dusk Till Dawn</u>, *Subliminal Cuts* are used to show but not reveal a bloody murder scene. In <u>The Bride Wore Black</u>, the camera *Subliminal Cuts* to Julie as she arrives at the doorway of her second victim's apartment.

In <u>The Graduate</u>, *Subliminal Cuts* are used as Mrs. Robinson attempts to seduce Benjamin with her body. In <u>Easy Rider</u>, many *Subliminal Cuts* are used as the riders are attacked in their sleep.

Subliminal Cut

CROSS CUT

What does it look like?

A *Cross Cut* cuts back and forth between separate scenes that are occurring in different places, usually at the same time. The camera alternates between multiple perspectives to show us the relationship between the scenes, increasing the drama of the events. *Cross Cuts* are often used to build tension and suspense.

An interesting way of stylizing *Cross Cuts* is to vary the camera speed in one of the scenes. One can be shot in slow motion while the other scene is filmed in real time. This makes the *Cross Cuts* more dramatic and interesting.

Where can I see it?

In A Better Tomorrow, John Woo cuts back and forth between the image of an assassin approaching his victims in slow motion and the victims sitting obliviously at a table in real time. Many gunfight sequences cut back and forth between the warring factions as they fight.

In Rocky, *Cross Cuts* contrast the training styles of Rocky and Apollo Creed. In Batman, the camera cuts between the Joker dancing and Batman fighting. In The Good, the Bad, and the Ugly, the camera *Cross Cuts* between soldiers marching, Clint Eastwood assembling his gun, and assassins approaching.

CROSS CUT

Cross Cuts

CUTAWAY

What does it look like?

A *Cutaway* is used in the film editing process to hide mistakes or to focus on interesting objects. This technique is simply a cut away from the main scene to an object within the scene— a prop for example. This object can be used as a "glue" to cut together two sequences that don't splice together smoothly.

The editor can compose the film in this order: Sequence 1, *Cutaway*, Sequence 2. Because the camera cuts away to an intermediate object, we don't notice the awkward transition between the two sequences.

A *Cutaway* can also emphasize images, objects, and characters within a scene.

Cutaway

FREEZE FRAME

What does it look like?

Quite simply, a *Freeze Frame* is a single frame of film played continuously to create the effect of a frozen image. The most frequent use of this technique is to end films on an enigmatic or emotional note.

Where can I see it?

*Freeze Frame*s are used to end <u>Butch Cassidy and the Sundance Kid</u>, <u>The Wild Bunch</u> and <u>Rocky</u>. <u>La Jetée</u> is a film that is composed almost entirely of photographic *Freeze Frames*. In <u>Goodfellas</u>, <u>Strictly Ballroom</u>, and <u>Out of Sight</u>, *Freeze Frames* are occasionally mixed in for effect.

Freeze Frame

LOOK AT

What does it look like?

Look At starts with an actor looking towards something offscreen. The camera then cuts to the object that is being looked at. The camera may then cut back to the actor for a reaction shot.

Look At illustrates an interesting aspect of film montage. While the actor and the object being looked at may be filmed hundreds of miles away from each other, the audience perceives the two elements as existing within the same physical space.

The order of the elements for this technique is very significant. By switching the reaction shot and the look shot, the emotional meaning of the scene is changed. For example: we first see a man driving along, and he looks happily out his window. The camera cuts to a devastating wreck on the side of the road and then cuts back to the driver to show his sympathetic reaction. If we reverse the order of the sequence, we end up with a man who is very sad until he sees a brutal car crash, and that makes him happy. This kind of association might give the audience the idea that the driver enjoys other peoples' pain. This is interesting because the footage didn't change— just the order in which it was presented.

Look At

MULTI-TAKE

What does it look like?

A *Multi-Take* referes to a single action that is repeated several times, from different angles and distances. The audience sees the same action occur, usually about two to three times. This adds dramatic impact to the scene.

A *Multi-Take* is used when an important or decisive action occurs in a film. Without this technique, the action might happen so quickly that the audience doesn't even notice. One solution would be to film it in slow motion, but the *Multi-Take* provides an effective alternative.

Where can I see it?

In <u>The Usual Suspects</u>, a coffee cup falls to the ground and shatters several times. In <u>The Killer</u>, John Woo *Multi-Takes* as an assassin pulls out his rifle to kill. In <u>The Color of Money</u>, the action of the cue hitting the pool ball is repeated from a few different angles for emphasis. Many martial arts movies use this technique to emphasize the punches and kicks in fight scenes. *Multi-Takes* appear at the end of <u>The Fury</u>, when Cassavetes' body explodes; in <u>Terminator 2: Judgment Day</u>, when the Terminator shatters the evil terminator's frozen body; and in <u>The Graduate</u>, when Ben spins around to look at Mrs. Robinson.

Multi-Take

CUT ZOOM IN

What does it look like?

Cut Zoom In is a technique that adds emphasis to an otherwise static shot. This technique usually has three stages: a very wide shot, a wide shot, and a medium shot. The distances for each shot can vary, but the basic idea is that, for each cut, the camera suddenly "jumps" forward towards the subject being viewed. To soften the effect, the camera can slowly zoom forward during the technique.

The two shot version of this technique is often used, but is not as distinct. A two shot *Cut Zoom In* consists of cutting from a wide shot to a close-up.

Where can I see it?

In <u>Die Hard 2</u>, Renny Harlin *Cut Zooms In* on the satellite dish just before it explodes. In <u>The Fifth Element</u>, Luc Besson performs a *Cut Zoom In* toward the headquarters of Zorg as Zorg speaks out his first, middle, and last names. In <u>La Femme Nikita</u>, there is a two shot *Cut Zoom In* when Nikita breaks open a bathroom window to prepare for an assassination. This two shot cut emphasizes the action. In <u>2001: A Space Odyssey</u>, the camera *Cut Zooms In* towards Hal's eye.

Cut Zoom In

CUT ZOOM OUT

What does it look like?

Cut Zoom Out is the opposite of Cut Zoom In. Instead of jumping closer to the subject, the camera moves farther away with each cut.

An example of a *Cut Zoom Out* sequence would be: close-up to wide shot to extremely long shot (establishing shot). The distance covered by a *Cut Zoom Out* is usually much farther than its counterpart.

The most common use of this technique is to show how far away something can be seen or heard. If something incredibly loud happens, the camera first shows where the sound originated. Then the camera zooms back to a location farther away where the audience still hears the sound. Finally, the camera moves to a location blocks or miles away where the sound can still be heard.

Where can I see it?

At the end of <u>The Matrix</u>, the camera *Cut Zooms Out* from the city.

Cut Zoom Out

MONTAGE SEQUENCE

What does it look like?

A *Montage Sequence* is a specific subset of montage. Many films contain these sequences that are often set to music. A *Montage Sequence* is used to conveniently express the passage of time or a sequence of events without dialogue. This technique involves the collection of many different visual images spliced together. The transitions between these images (fades, cuts, dissolves) can greatly affect the emotional impact of the sequence.

Where can I see it?

In <u>Rocky</u>, a *Montage Sequence* shows Rocky training for his big fight. <u>NYPD Blue</u> has an opening credits *Montage Sequence* that shows establishing shots of New York. <u>Butch Cassidy and the Sundance Kid</u> has a bicycle-riding *Montage Sequence*. In the beginning of <u>Mimic</u>, a *Montage Sequence* presents the images that fade in and out to present an ominous, chilling introduction. In <u>Easy Rider</u>, several *Montage Sequences* show the characters driving across the country.

Montage Sequence

JUMP CUT SEQUENCE

What does it look like?

A *Jump Cut Sequence* is a specific type of Montage Sequence in which jump cuts are used to show similar actions occurring over a short period of time. What makes this technique different from other Montage Sequences is that the camera focuses on one particular scene or character, using jump cuts to create a sequence. The camera alternates between close-ups and wide shots, changing the angle slightly for each take. Jump cuts add energy to a character's actions.

Where can I see it?

In <u>Kiss the Girls</u>, a *Jump Cut Sequence* shows Ashley Judd practicing her kickboxing techniques. In <u>Sex, Lies, and Videotape</u>, a *Jump Cut Sequence* shows Graham destroying his collection of video tapes.

Jump Cut Sequence

SPLIT SCREEN

What does it look like?

A *Split Screen* shows two separate sequences on the screen at the same time. For example: the image can be split down the middle, allowing one scene to occur on the left side and another to occur on the right. The frame may be split into halves, quarters, whatever, depending on what the director needs.

Where can I see it?

Both <u>When Harry Met Sally</u> and <u>Indiscreet</u> use a *Split Screen* as two lovers talk on the phone. At the end of <u>Carrie</u>, *Split Screen* showcases the hellish prom disaster.

Split Screen

SUB-CLIP

What does it look like?

A *Sub-Clip* is similar to the picture-in-picture effect that high-end television owners have experienced. *Sub-Clips* help to show a new camera shot without cutting away.

Instead of cutting to a new shot, the *Sub-Clip* opens on top of the main scene and plays through. This technique often illustrates some relevant information, such as what a character is looking at.

Where can I see it?

In The Andromeda Strain, when research scientists come into the town, they go door to door, looking for survivors. Instead of cutting to the inside of each house as they look in, *Sub-Clips* open on the screen to show the ravaged bodies inside.

In Knock Off, a *Sub-Clip* opens as Van Damme looks into a box of knock-off goods. *Sub-Clips* open in Buffalo '66, as Billy thinks about his childhood.

Sub-Clip

SUPERIMPOSITION

What does it look like?

Superimposition adds supporting imagery to a scene. This technique is accomplished by overlaying a scene with a secondary image that is semitransparent.

The secondary image adds to the atmosphere. For example: if a director wants to show that a character is thinking about a long lost loved one, the image of the loved one's close-up can be *Superimposed* over the scene.

Where can I see it?

In <u>The Tin Drum</u>, the image of a young boy banging on his drum is *Superimposed* over a scene in which he is born.

Superimposition

FILL, REVEAL FRAME

What does it look like?

Fill, Reveal Frame allows the director to cut without the audience knowing it. This technique can be used to create jumps in space and time within a film.

If the camera is moving, it may move in front of a wall or some other object that obscures the camera's view. If the object is dark enough, the director can fool the audience by cutting to another shot where the camera is moving away from a different dark object. The cut happens so transparently that the audience may not notice unless they are paying very close attention.

Another variation is a person or object moving into the camera frame. Because that object blocks the light from the camera, the audience can't tell when a cut is made to the object at a completely different location. The object can then be moved away from the lens to reveal the new scene.

Where can I see it?

Fill, Reveal Frame is used throughout <u>Rope</u> to hide the few cuts that exist.

Fill, Reveal Frame

WALK, REVEAL FRAME

What does it look like?

Walk, Reveal Frame is a clever transition technique. It starts out with an actor walking in front of the camera. As the actor passes in front of the lens, the audience's view becomes partially obscured. This allows the editor to cut to a new shot without the audience noticing. When the actor walks away, the camera position has changed.

Where can I see it?

Jaws uses this technique several times before a shark attack at the beach. The Usual Suspects cuts as a character paces back and forth in front of the camera.

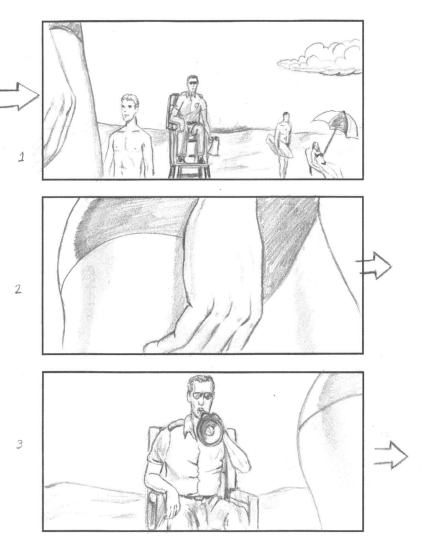

Walk, Reveal Frame

COLLAGE

What does it look like?

    Collage involves composing small, moving images onto the screen. These images usually consist of imagery that enhances a story's thematic context. The images look as if they were pasted into place, similar to how a collage looks in real life. This is done during the editing process after filming is finished.

Where can I see it?

    In <u>Ed Wood</u>, Ed Wood's ideas are displayed as *Collage* elements. In <u>Drugstore Cowboy</u>, various random images float across the screen to simulate Bob's drug-induced state.

Collage

CAMERA SNAP

What does it look like?

A *Camera Snap* gives us a character's perspective when looking through a camera and taking pictures. At first, we see the world from a distance— through the camera lens. As the character presses a button, a snapping sound is played and the images freeze, as if they had just been captured on film. Shortly after, reality starts moving again and this process continues as long as pictures are taken.

A variation on this technique is to show a flash effect just before the freeze frame, to simulate the camera's flash.

Where can I see it?

Camera Snap is used in <u>Thelma and Louise</u>, when the two women take a picture of themselves.

Camera Snap

PHOTO TO SCENE

What does it look like?

When a character has just seen a picture or a photograph of a far-away place, a director can use *Photo To Scene* for a clever transition, filling the frame with the photograph, and then dissolving to the actual subject of the photograph, shot from approximately the same angle and distance. The abstract representation becomes reality.

Where can I see it?

At the end of <u>Fletch</u>, the scene dissolves from a photograph of the beach to a live shot from the same angle and distance.

Photo To Scene

IMPACT FLASH, FLASHED CUT, FLASHED JUMP CUT

What does it look like?

Impact Flashes look similar to photographic bulbs being flashed. This technique is very popular in commercials and music videos, to add impact to a scene.

In a *Flashed Cut*, the camera flashes to white. The film cuts to a different frame during the flash. The flash then dies down, revealing a new image.

Flashed Jump Cut is the same as a *Flashed Cut*, but is used specifically to emphasize a jump cut.

Flashed Cut

EXERCISES

• **Practice editing techniques.** Professional editing systems can cost as much as $100,000 or more. However, as technology progresses, lower cost video editing alternatives are being made available to consumers who want to edit their home videos and who don't care that the finished product is not broadcast quality. If you're interested in setting up a video editing system, look at some of the lower end video capture cards to get started. You may even be able to use a pair of cheap VCRs to do some simple editing by dubbing from one to the other.

• **Edit "in camera."** What this means is that instead of composing the footage in a video editor, you'll capture the images in sequence on film. This very difficult technique requires that you plan everything ahead of time and that you don't make any mistakes when shooting.

• **Watch movies and observe the rhythm of the edits.** How fast are they? What does the editor cut to? Are there certain patterns? How does the editing affect the scene? Think of ways you might have edited the scene differently and try to visualize what it would have looked like.

• **Write shooting scripts for a small film you want to make.** A shooting script lists the shots that will appear on screen when the audience watches the film. Once again, learn to visualize the final product before you spend time, energy, and money to create it.

MISCELLANEOUS TECHNIQUES

There are a number of cinematic techniques that don't fit into a neat package, but are still very interesting to learn. These "miscellaneous" techniques are included here.

SLOW MOTION, FAST MOTION, MOTION MIXER

What does it look like?

Changing the camera's filming speed can create surrealistic effects. By filming at more than 24 frames per second, *Slow Motion* is achieved. *Slow Motion* extends the length of a shot, adding intensity to a scene. By playing the action out slowly, the audience has more time to savor what is happening.

Fast Motion is just the opposite. By filming at less than 24 frames per second, the images onscreen speed up. This is often used for comic effect, or to "fast forward" through a scene. Some directors will change the speed of the camera over time. This results in a scene that alternates between *Slow Motion*, regular motion, and *Fast Motion* for an added effect. I call this the *Motion Mixer*.

Where can I see it?

Many action movies by directors such as Sam Peckinpah, John Woo, and Luc Besson add *Slow Motion* shots to action sequences in order to extend their dramatic impact. John Woo uses *Slow Motion* in A Better Tomorrow, The Killer, and Face/Off. In El Mariachi, *Fast Motion* is used when a solo mariachi plays his keyboard.

In Baz Luhrmann's Romeo + Juliet, the *Motion Mixer* is used. Both *Fast Motion* and *Slow Motion* appear in The Color of Money, as the characters play pool. In The Untouchables, *Slow Motion* intensifies a gunfight between Elliot and the gangsters as a baby's stroller spins out of control down the stairs. At the end of Bonnie and Clyde, the deaths of the two main characters are filmed partially in *Slow Motion*.

SPLIT FOCUS

What does it look like?

Like our eyes, camera lenses have the ability to focus only on a certain field of objects. We experience this when we try to look at something close. If our eyes do not adjust, the image of the closest object will be blurry. The camera can eliminate this blurriness by pulling focus, causing the foreground objects to gain sharpness and the background objects to become blurred.

Split Focus relies on a device called a split-field diopter. A diopter splits the focus on each side of the lens. This allows one side of the lens to be focused on something far in the background, while the other side is focused on something up close.

Where can I see it?

Split Focus

The Fury gives us a close-up of a young woman in bed and a nurse watching in the background. In Raising Cain, *Split Focus* shows a detective in the foreground while Cain sits in the background answering questions. Brian De Palma uses this technique in many of his films.

CHROMA KEYING

What does it look like?

Chroma Keying easily replaces a section of a scene with another image. This technique may be used to show a character in a dangerous or impossible situation without the actor ever being there.

An actor is filmed against a colored wall that is usually completely green or completely blue. Because the wall is a single color, a computer can remove the background by removing that color. The computer can then paste the actor onto a new background. This technique may also be used to replace objects within a scene. In post-production, patches of greenscreen in a scene can be used as areas that need to be replaced.

Where can I see it?

In <u>Superman</u>, the scenes of Superman flying were shot against a greenscreen and then composited onto a film image of the sky moving by.

Chroma Keying

COLOR SEEP

What does it look like?

Color Seep is a technique in which an image's saturation is changed over time. The saturation of an image determines how much color it has. An oversaturated image will look unnaturally bright and washed out. An image with the saturation removed becomes black and white. This process either gradually removes the saturation from a color image, or gradually adds saturation to a black and white image, ending up in color.

Where can I see it?

Watch <u>Platoon</u>. After the final battle, the camera pans over a black and white landscape and gradually fades into color. <u>Butch Cassidy and the Sundance Kid</u> starts out in sepia-toned black and white. After the introduction, the image fades into color. Then at the end of the movie, the image loses its saturation once again.

JOURNEY THROUGH EYE

What does it look like?

Journey Through Eye transitions from the real world into a character's inner thoughts. The camera moves toward an extreme close-up of a character's eye and then dissolves to a scene that represents that character's subconscious. The technique can be reversed—to transition from a character's subconscious to conscious reality.

Where can I see it?

In <u>Contact</u>, the camera pulls through the universe and journeys through Ellie's eyes. In <u>Highlander</u>, the camera pulls through the eye of Connor MacLeod, transitioning from his past into the present.

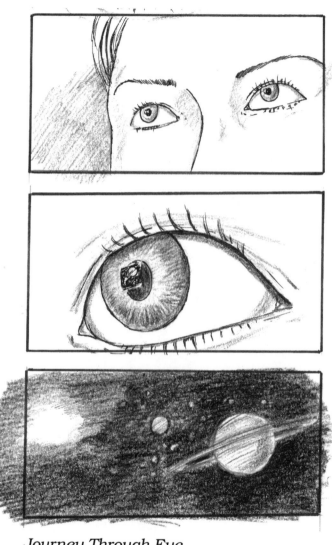

Journey Through Eye

REAR PROJECTION

What does it look like?

Rear Projection is the process of projecting a film image onto a screen behind the actors. If done correctly, the audience sees both the scene in progress and the projected images blended together seamlessly. The effect can be very surreal. *Rear Projection* gives the impression that a separate universe is happening alongside the real universe, both in the same scene.

Before audiences became as sophisticated as they are today, actors in older movies often sat in a model car and pretended to drive. Behind them, a *Rear Projection* showed images of streets and cars moving by. Because this looks fake to our modern eyes, *Rear Projection* is seldom used anymore for traveling shots, and is most often used as a special effect.

Where can I see it?

Rear Projection is used several times in <u>Austin Powers: The Spy Who Shagged Me</u> to give us the feeling of old movies.

Rear Projection

GLOBAL ZOOM

What does it look like?

A *Global Zoom* begins with an establishing shot of an entire planet. The camera then zooms, via a digital effect, toward the planet until it finally reaches the surface. This technique, used in reverse, adds finality to a scene or to the entire film.

Where can I see it?

The 'Burbs uses this technique and its reversal to begin and end the film.

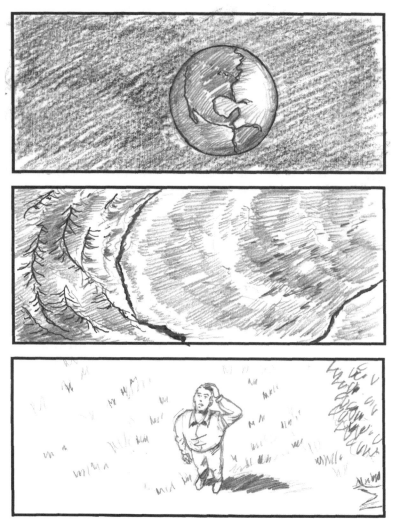

Global Zoom

SLICE OF LIFE

What does it look like?

The *Slice Of Life* shows a "slice" of life, frozen in time or at extremely slow speeds, from many different angles.

A series of photographic cameras are set up up at varying angles around the subject of interest. All of the cameras are then fired at a programmed speed to capture the subject from several different angles at the desired instant. The still images are spliced together. Finally, a computer creates in-betweens for the images to eliminate jitters.

Where can I see it?

The Matrix uses *Slice Of Life* several times to show characters doing impossible things like dodging bullets. *Slice Of Life* can be seen in Lost in Space, when the spacecraft enters hyperdrive. Commercials and music videos use this technique occasionally.

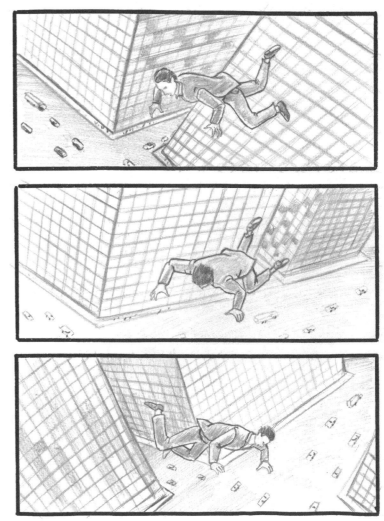

Slice Of Life

STROBE

What does it look like?

Strobe adds pulsating imagery to a scene. Similar to a disco, the lights flash on and off, providing discrete glimpses of the action.

Where can I see it?

In Jacob's Ladder, Strobe intensifies the nightmarish imagery during a bizarre party scene.

Strobe

THEMATIC FILTER, NEGATIVE

What does it look like?

A filter is one of many tools available to a filmmaker for altering a film's final appearance. Filters are colored sheets or colored panes of glass that change the color of light that passes through. Filters are often placed over lighting equipment to change the color of light being projected, and over camera lenses to change the color of light caught on film. Common uses of filters include: making the sunset look more golden, reducing the reflection of windows, and warming the skin tones of the actors.

A *Thematic Filter* filters out an entire range of colors, leaving an image saturated heavily by a single hue. This leftover color range sets the mood for the scene in which it is used.

A *Negative* is similar to the *Thematic Filter* for black and white films. A *Negative* is simply a reversal of the colors. Shades of black become white and vice versa.

Where can I see it?

Negative is used several times towards the end of Godard's <u>Alphaville</u>. In <u>Natural Born Killers</u>, the color of lime green is used as a common theme throughout the film. *Thematic Filters* are used in several scenes to filter the light, giving it a distinct lime green appearance.

IMAGERY

What does it look like?

The concept of *Imagery* in a film can mean many different things. *Imagery* can be used to emphasize emotional elements of a scene without any dialogue. For example: in a scene where the characters are talking about war, stock footage of violent battles may be intercut with the conversation. This is a good use of *Imagery*.

In a more general sense, *Imagery* represents any collection of images (montage) that affects the audience on a purely emotional level. Images tend to have certain associated meanings. A flower might signify peace or love, and a gun might signify war. Images that contradict their natural meanings can be even more interesting. For example: a beautiful, but poisonous flower.

Where can I see it?

All of David Lynch's films use *Imagery* extensively. My personal favorite is Lost Highway, but I would recommend watching them all. In Marathon Man, images of a champion marathon runner are used. In Apocalypse Now, the *Imagery* of rotating helicopter blades is blended with the *Imagery* of a spinning ceiling fan.

In Spellbound, *Imagery* represents a dream sequence that was inspired by the paintings of Salvador Dali. Battleship Potemkin uses *Images* of sailors hanging from the mast. Jacob's Ladder has many scenes of nightmarish *Imagery*. In M, the *Imagery* of a child's ball rolling out from the forest signifies her death.

KINETIC ENERGY

What does it look like?

According to physics, *Kinetic Energy* is the energy of motion. In the realm of filmmaking, *Kinetic Energy* describes the motion of the camera in a scene. There are an infinite number of ways to move a camera, and each one has a unique impact on an audience. Some examples of *Kinetic Energy* are: dolly movements, Steadicam™ sequences, handheld shots, crane moves, and jib paths.

The shakes that result from handheld camera work add energy to a scene. Steadicams™ can be used for sequences that require a wide range of movement while maintaining a very smooth image. Mechanical devices such as cranes, jibs, and dollies usually create smooth camera movements that are constrained to the device's limits.

An inventive example of *Kinetic Energy* is to place the camera on a swing, a merry-go-round, a roller coaster, or any object that has its own unique type of movement.

Where can I see it?

In Straw Dogs, Peckinpah uses a handheld camera to add energy to the action scenes. In Rosemary's Baby, a handheld camera observes Rosemary as she struggles to escape. Breaking the Waves has a considerable amount of *Kinetic Energy*. In The Good, the Bad, and the Ugly, the camera spins quickly as a character searches through a cemetery for gold. Handheld cameras are used during a chase sequence in Planet of the Apes.

As interesting as it can be, *Kinetic Energy* is not everything. For most of The Godfather, the camera is very still. This lack of rapid camera movement does not detract at all from the power of the film's drama.

LENS

What does it look like?

When shooting a film, a camera *Lens* can have a great deal of impact on the mood and quality of the final image. A wide angle lens sees more of a landscape, but distorts objects that are close to the camera. This distortion can be to the director's advantage, perhaps if they are looking for a psychedelic mood for their film. An extreme wide angle lens has much more noticeable distortion. These lenses are sometimes referred to as fisheye lenses.

The focal length of a lens determines its viewing area. A short focal length indicates a wide angle lens, while a long focal length indicates a telephoto lens. Lenses with long focal lengths allow the camera to be positioned far away from the subject being filmed. These lenses have the effect of compressing the image depth, making objects in the frame appear closer to each other than they actually are. This compression is often good for stunts, by making the stunt players look much closer to dangerous explosions and car chases than they are.

Another interesting property of lenses is that they change the perceived speed at which characters move onscreen. Through a telephoto lens actors walking perpendicular to the camera appear to be moving faster. Through a wide angle lens actors walking toward the camera appear to be moving faster.

MIXED MEDIA

What does it look like?

Mixed Media is the result of mixing the traditional film medium (filming live actors, sets, and props) with other media such as animation, drawings, and photographs. Computer-generated imagery and optical printers aside, traditional filmmaking's constraint is that it can film only what is reality. A camera can't capture an imaginary image. By using other types of media, filmmakers may accomplish cinematic techniques that are impossible by traditional means.

Mixed Media can express what may be too expensive to re-create in reality. Scenes with extremely complex movement and interaction might be less expensive to animate than to film. Low budget films may use pictures and drawings to symbolize large-scale sequences.

Where can I see it?

In <u>Who Framed Roger Rabbit</u> and <u>Cool World</u>, animated characters interact with their live action counterparts. In <u>Tank Girl</u>, comic book snippets and animation segments are interspersed with live action. In <u>Once Upon a Time in the West</u>, a painting of the ocean is used to signify the railroad tycoon's unachievable goal of reaching the Pacific Ocean.

MIXING STOCKS

What does it look like?

There are many different types of film that a filmmaker can choose. Each type is called a film stock, and its unique physical characteristics determine how the final image will look. In addition, there are many different formats for film: 8mm (used for home movies before video camcorders), 16mm (used for documentaries, low budget films), and 35mm (used for most feature films). I also include video, since many directors have experimented with mixing video with filmed images or filming with nothing but video cameras. While other film formats exist that are used for large-screen theaters, these formats are usually too cumbersome for mainstream cinema.

Each film format defines the film's frame size. The larger the frame size, the greater the detail that can be captured, resulting in better image quality. By mixing these formats within a movie, a filmmaker can achieve varying levels of perception, based on the way the image texture changes.

Where can I see it?

Several of Oliver Stone's films *Mix Stocks*. In <u>Drugstore Cowboy</u>, we see 8mm home movies. In <u>The Game</u>, 16mm film is used to create flashback sequences to the character's childhood.

SOUND DESIGN,
VOICEOVER

What does it look like?

Although *Sound Design* is not a visual cinematic technique, we must keep in mind that movies are an audio-visual medium. *Sound Design* is an incredibly important aspect of the cinematic experience. Imagine what Star Wars would be like without music. It would lose much of its grandeur. If you stripped a horror movie of its bombastic *Sound Design*, it would probably lose its ability to frighten us. Music goes a long way towards setting the mood for a scene, but even more subtle and powerful are the sounds that the audience doesn't notice. It is not uncommon for films to add sounds as enhancements in post-production: birds singing, cars driving by, water running. *Sound Design* can enhance or detract from an audience's enjoyment of a film.

A *Voiceover* is a specific aspect of *Sound Design* employed in many films. This technique involves dubbing a character or a narrator's voice over a scene as a means of narration.

Where can I see it?

A very powerful example of sound design happens in <u>The Godfather</u>. As Michael Corleone prepares to murder his first victims, the sound of a rushing train fades in and out to signify the ebb and flow of his emotions. As he walks out into the diner to make the kill, the sound of the train floods the scene.

In any movie with music, observe how the music affects the mood of the scene. In <u>The Graduate</u>, the music slows down as Ben's car runs out of gas. In many horror movies, bombastic sound effects are used to emphasize horrifying and surprising moments. <u>Goodfellas</u> is partially narrated by a Ray Liotta *Voiceover*. In <u>Duel</u>, the character's thoughts are vocalized as a *Voiceover*. The beginning of <u>Citizen Kane</u> is narrated by a *Voiceover*.

CGI CINEMA

What does it look like?

CGI stands for "computer-generated imagery." As computers become more powerful and sophisticated, their ability to generate lifelike creatures, models, and special effects improves. The number of films that rely on computer graphics is steadily increasing each year.

CGI Cinema allows filmmakers to achieve complex cinematic movements that are not possible in the real world. In a virtual world, the camera can move anywhere and at any speed. This kind of control allows for the introduction of many new and exciting additions to the cinematic palette available to filmmakers.

Where can I see it?

<u>Jurassic Park</u> and <u>Terminator 2: Judgment Day</u> are just two well known examples of breakthroughs in mainstream computer-generated imagery for films. In <u>Forrest Gump</u>, computer effects are used in subtle ways that are almost transparent to the audience. A feather that floats to the ground is computer generated, and the "legless" Vietnam veteran had his legs removed inside a computer.

EXERCISES

• **Study cinema.** Now it's time for you to start doing your own cinematic research. With a new perspective, watch movies that you've seen several times before. Watch those you don't think you will like— you may find new "flavors" of filmmaking that you never knew existed. Keep an eye out for commonly used cinematic techniques and try to invent your own. Study directing, filmmaking, cinema. Learn common techniques and common mistakes. A great deal of knowledge can be gained by studying the work of artists before you.

SUMMARY

If you're a filmmaker, perhaps you can use the knowledge here to further hone your technical skills. If you're a film buff, you may have been motivated to watch movies you wouldn't have dared to look at before. If you are new to film studies, we hope you've been inspired to look more deeply into movies you used to take for granted.

Regardless, we sincerely hope that this book has increased your love and understanding of films.

Jeremy Vineyard, Author

Jose Cruz, Illustrator

ABOUT THE AUTHORS

Jeremy Vineyard, Author

Jeremy Vineyard is a writer and an avid student of film. Based in Southern California, Jeremy continues to work towards his goal of directing feature films as well as pursuing a professional writing career. As an artist, he hopes to teach through his nonfiction writing and to tell stories through filmmaking, animation, graphic novels, and other creative venues.

Jose Cruz, Illustrator

Jose Cruz is a professional illustrator and storyboard artist. He has worked on several feature films, short films, animated shorts, and international commercials. His passion for art is surpassed only by his love for the art of filmmaking. Jose hopes to continue working in films as a storyboard artist and an art director. He also plans to produce film and television content for American-Hispanic audiences in the near future.

MOVIES REFERENCE

This section contains a list of all the movies that were mentioned this book, along with their corresponding director(s).

2001: A Space Odyssey: **20, 74, 89**
Stanley Kubrick

Ace Ventura: Pet Detective: **68**
Tom Shadyac

After Hours: **44, 54**
Martin Scorsese

Aliens: **68**
James Cameron

Alphaville: **113**
Jean-Luc Godard

The Andromeda Strain: **94**
Robert Wise

Apocalypse Now: **114**
Francis Coppola

Army of Darkness: **54, 67**
Sam Raimi

Austin Powers: The Spy Who Shagged Me: **109**
Jay Roach

Batman: **26, 71, 76, 83**
Batman Returns
Tim Burton

Battleship Potemkin: **114**
Grigori Aleksandrov
Sergei M. Eisenstein

A Better Tomorrow: **83, 104**
John Woo

Blade Runner: **45**
Ridley Scott

Blue: **58, 59**
Krzysztof Kieslowski

Blue Velvet: **55**
David Lynch

visualize quick with
StoryBoard Quick
(Even if you can't draw.)

You don't have to know how to draw to create the shot setup you see in your mind's eye. Simply choose from the built-in characters, locations and props. Move them around in the frame into the desired set up....zoom to a CU, rotate the character into an over-the-shoulder, open the capiton window and add your dialog. It's the fastest way to storyboard...even if you can draw!

StoryBoard Quick™

Available for WINDOWS and MACINTOSH

StoryBoard Quick's easy to use interface makes creating each frame a snap. Choose your aspect ratio and start boarding. Import digital location shots and layer the characters and props on top. Create spatial relationships with ease. Create new frames with a click... No more stick figures, no more erasing.

• layer control • zoom in and out •
preset aspect ratios
people • places • props
• storyboard templates • caption box •

- Character positions: running, sitting, jumping, prone and standing; male and female generic characters.
- Props -includes kids & animals.
- New Location images.
- Pop up grids full of images ready for use at point and click command.
- Add on character libraries with attitude!
- Quick drag-and-drop importing!

Print and you're on your way to the set! Choose from numerous pre-defined storyboard layouts. If you're the visionary...let them see what you think before they start telling you... Get your ideas onto paper Quick!

PowerProduction Software

visit our website for online demo of
StoryBoard Quick and StoryBoard Artist
www.powerproduction.com

From the industry leader in worldwide production planning. PowerProduction Software has software to fit your needs.

Call 1.800.457.0383
or 408 358-2358

THE INDEPENDENT FILM & VIDEOMAKER'S GUIDE
2ND EDITION

Michael Wiese

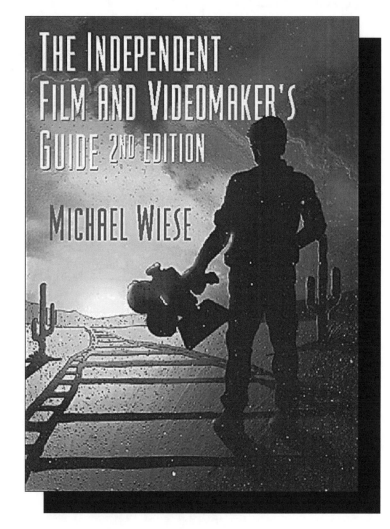

Wiese has packed 25 years of experience in film and video into the most comprehensive and most useful book ever for filmmakers seeking both independence and success in the marketplace. Loaded with insider's tips to help filmmakers avoid the pitfalls of show business, this book is the equivalent of a "street smart degree" in filmmaking.

This new, completely expanded and revised edition has all the information you need, from raising the cash through distribution, that caused the original edition to sell more than 35,000 copies.

Contents include writing mission statements, developing your ideas into concepts, scriptwriting, directing, producing, market research, the distribution markets (theatrical, home video, television, international), financing your film, pitching, presentations, writing a business plan, and a huge appendix filled with film cash flow projections, sample contracts, valuable contact addresses, and much more.

> *"A straightfoward and clear overview on the business of making films or videos. Wiese covers the most important (and least taught) part of the job: creative deal-making. The book is full of practical tips on how to get a film or video project financed, produced, and distributed without sacrificing artistic integrity. A must for any aspiring independent producer."*
>
> **Co-Evolution Quarterly** (about the first edition)

$29.95, Approx. 500 pages, over 300 illustrations, 6 x 8-1/4
ISBN 0-941188-57-4
Order # 37RLS

To order this book for classroom use, please call Focal Press at 1-800-366-2665.

SCREENWRITING 101
THE ESSENTIAL CRAFT OF FEATURE FILM WRITING
Neill D. Hicks

NEW!

This book provides writers with the tools necessary to write and market a successful screenplay.

"Having a great idea is not enough. You need to get it down on the page. Having a great script is not enough. You have to pitch it to the right person at the right moment in time!" says Hicks.

Elements include:
- Structure
- Characters
- Style
- The Business of Screenwriting
- The Economics of Film
- Agents, Attorneys, and the Screenwriter
- And much more!

NEILL D. HICKS' credits include two of the number one box office films in the world—*Rumble in the Bronx* in the United States and *First Strike* in Asia. Some of his other Hollywood screenwriting credits include the critically acclaimed *Dead Reckoning*, starring Cliff Robertson, and *Don't Talk to Strangers,* starring Pierce Brosnan.

Movie Entertainment Book Club Selection

NEILL D. HICKS teaches screenwriting workshops throughout the United States, Canada, and Europe.

$16.95, 200 pages, 6 x 9
ISBN 0-941188-72-8
Order # 41RLS

FILM DIRECTING - SHOT BY SHOT:
VISUALIZING FROM CONCEPT TO SCREEN

by Steven D. Katz

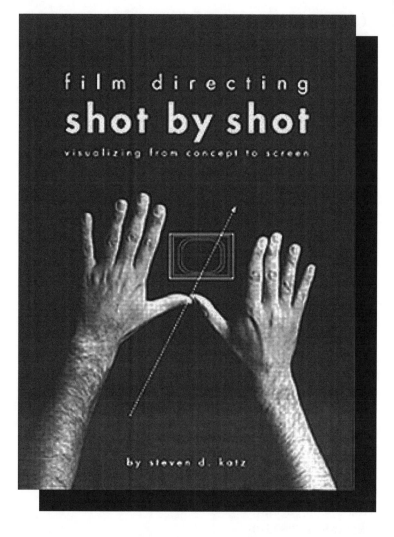

FILM DIRECTING SHOT BY SHOT is a complete catalogue of visual techniques and their stylistic implications for both film and video directors—a "textbook" which enables working filmmakers (as well as screenwriters and producers) to expand their stylistic knowledge.

Extensively illustrated and well-written, it should find an enthusiastic audience among both seasoned and novice filmmakers.

Includes illustrations, photos and storyboards from:

• Alfred Hitchcock's *THE BIRDS* and *TORN CURTAIN*

• Steven Spielberg's *EMPIRE OF THE SUN*

• Orson Welles' *CITIZEN KANE*

• N.C. Wyeth and Howard Pyle artwork

• David Byrne's illustrations from *TRUE STORIES*

Contents include: Camera Techniques, Storyboard Style, Screen Ballistics, Framing and Compositional Techniques, Graphic Properties, Lenses, Moving Cameras, Style, How Directors Interpret Script Scenes, Blocking, Editing and Transitions, Image Organization, Symbolic Meaning, and Modern Techniques.

$24.95, 370 pages, 7 x 10
Approx. 400 illus. and photos
ISBN 0-941188-10-8
Order # 7RLS

THE WRITER'S JOURNEY
MYTHIC STRUCTURE FOR WRITERS - 2ND EDITION

Christopher Vogler

This new edition provides fresh insights and observations from Vogler's ongoing work with mythology's influence on stories, movies, and humankind itself.

Learn why thousands of professional writers have made THE WRITER'S JOURNEY a best-seller and why it is considered required reading by many of Hollywood's top studios! Learn how master storytellers have used mythic structure to create powerful stories that tap into the mythological core which exists in us all.

Writers of both fiction and nonfiction will discover a set of useful myth-inspired storytelling paradigms (e.g., The Hero's Journey) and step-by-step guidelines to plot and character development. Based on the work of Joseph Campbell, THE WRITER'S JOURNEY is a must for writers of all kinds.

• A foreword describing the worldwide reaction to the first edition and the continued influence of The Hero's Journey model.

• Vogler's new observations on the adaptability of THE WRITER'S JOURNEY for international markets, and the changing profile of the audience.

• The latest observations and techniques for using the mythic model to enhance modern storytelling.

• New subject index and filmography.

• How to apply THE WRITER'S JOURNEY paradigm to your own life.

Book-of-the-Month Club Selection • Writer's Digest Book Club Selection
Movie Entertainment Book Club Selection

$22.95, 300 pages, 6 x 9
ISBN 0-941188-70-1
Order # 2598RLS

New analyses of box office blockbusters such as Titanic, The Lion King, The Full Monty, Pulp Fiction, and Star Wars.

MICHAEL WIESE PRODUCTIONS
11288 VENTURA BLVD., #821

Studio City, CA 91604

1-818-379-8799

kenlee@earthlink.net

www.mwp.com

Please send me the following books:

Title   *Order Number (#RLS___)*   *Amount*

_____   _____

_____   _____

_____   _____

SHIPPING   _____

California Tax (8.25%)   _____

TOTAL ENCLOSED   _____

Please make check or money order payable to *Michael Wiese Productions*

(Check one) ☐ MasterCard ☐ Visa ☐ AmEx

Credit Card Number _____ Expiration Date _____

Cardholder's Name _____

Cardholder's Signature _____

SHIPPING

All orders must be prepaid

UPS GROUND SERVICE
One Item - $7.00
Each Add'l Item, add $2

SPECIAL REPORTS - $2 EACH
Express - 3 Business Days
add $12 per Order

OVERSEAS
Surface - $15.00 each item
Airmail - $30.00 each item

SHIP TO:

Name _____

Address _____

City _____ State _____ Zip _____

Write or Fax for a free catalog

HOW TO ORDER:

1 CALL 24 HOURS
7 DAYS A WEEK

2 CREDIT CARD ORDERS
CALL 1-800-833-5738

3 OR FAX YOUR ORDER
818-986-3408

4 OR MAIL THIS
FORM